A Schoolboy's War in Essex

A SCHOOLBOY'S WAR IN ESSEX

DAVID F. WOOD

The
History
Press

First published 2010

The History Press
The Mill, Brimscombe Port
Stroud, Gloucestershire, GL5 2QG
www.thehistorypress.co.uk

British Library Cataloguing in Publication Data.
A catalogue record for this book is available from the British Library.

ISBN 978 0 7524 5517 4

Typesetting and origination by The History Press
Printed in India, Aegean Offset
Manufacturing managed by jellyfish Print Solutions Ltd

This is for my children and grandchildren; I hope they will read this book and in doing so get some understanding of what life was really like in those dark days which are now history.

ACKNOWLEDGEMENTS

As I started to write this book I realised the enormous influence that my parents and my three aunts had exercised over my formative years. Sadly, only one member of that generation survives and my first thanks must be to my dear Auntie Lill, who showed such care and patience in helping me learn to read, ride my bicycle, and acquire a basic knowledge of French. Above all, she was always there.

I would also like to thank Carole, my wife, who encouraged me to write this book and was always there with suggestions and encouragement when I questioned what had ever got me started on this project.

I have to acknowledge the support which I received from the team at The History Press. In particular Sophie Bradshaw, who encouraged me to start this project and overcome my doubts about my ability to create a readable narrative. Also to Rich Saunders, whose constructive comments were invaluable in the editing and final stages.

CONTENTS

I

THE TEMPESTUOUS THIRTIES

When historians come to write the history of the twentieth century, the 1930s will surely be seen as one of the most tempestuous of its decades.

Britain, and indeed the whole of Europe, had emerged bloodied from the First World War and those who returned to this country found only poverty and unemployment as their reward for five years of hell in the trenches. The class system had broken down and although seen by many as a good thing, it left the working and ruling classes in unknown territory. Centuries of 'knowing their place' had been swept aside and the future became uncertain for landowner and farm labourer alike.

The younger generation entered the 1920s with great gusto and abandon, indulging in all sorts of excesses, presumably in an attempt to wash away the horror of the war years. A by-product of the war was a severe shortage of eligible young men, which created a problem for those women of marriageable age seeking husbands. It also had an effect on the employment market, creating a gap in the professional occupations, such as law and medicine. However, the depression and massive strikes in the late 1920s led to polarisation of political thought, giving rise to fascism and communism at the same time.

This was not, of course, confined to Britain; similar things were happening across Europe. Stalin was tightening his grip in the East and Franco, Mussolini and Hitler were preparing to take Western Europe down the fascist path.

1931 saw a National Government led by Ramsay MacDonald, the abolition of the gold standard and the founding of the British Union of Fascists under Oswald Moseley. By the mid-thirties we saw the first fascist rallies in London and the storm clouds were gathering over Europe. Hitler had been appointed as Chancellor in Germany and he very quickly established a reign of terror, including the creation of concentration camps. Jews were gradually disenfranchised and those who saw the future with clarity made their escape to Britain or America; some even went to Israel but the vast majority of Jews did not see the danger until it was too late.

But I knew none of this as I entered the world in late 1934. I was born in a nursing home in Underwood Street, Hoxton, one foggy November evening, the only son to Donald and Debby Wood. We lived in a one-bedroom flat at No. 24 East Road. We shared a sink and cold water on the landing with the flat above and the communal toilet was in the yard on the ground floor. Beneath us was a dentist's surgery and I often heard the screams of patients echoing up the stairs. Anaesthetics as we know them today were virtually non-existent.

My father was a cabinet maker and had a workshop which he shared with his younger brother, Jack, in Pitfield Street. My mother's family – her father who had fled the pogroms in Russia at the turn of the century and two of her three sisters, Betty and Lilly – lived a few doors along at No. 16 East Road. Opposite was Dawson's department store, a prominent North London landmark.

Betty had worked for Greenfields, a local hat factory, since leaving school, as had my mother prior to my arrival. Lilly had been forced to leave school at fourteen to care for my grandfather, who was a widower and blind. She had a talent for dressmaking and established a very successful business in what was probably the first floor parlour, employing staff including my mother, who worked part-time, and an old family friend, Minnie Levy. I used to enjoy going with Mum to Auntie Lill's because I got to spend time with my grandfather, who would recount stories of life in Russia when he was a young man. Anti-Semitism under the Czar was rife and the Jews were treated very harshly. There were periodic raids by the local soldiers and they would run down anyone unfortunate enough to stand in their way. Houses would be burnt and livestock slaughtered. My grandmother's own brother was killed during one of these attacks and she was left for dead. She died at a very young age, probably as a result of the ordeal she suffered and, of course, bearing six children, one of whom had died when he was about a year old.

My mother had two other siblings, Harry, who was married to Kitty, and Jane, who was the youngest and worked as a live-in nanny for a family in Tottenham. Harry and Kitty had a daughter, Doris, who was a few months older than me and a son, Alan, born in 1938. The family did not like Kitty and, in fact, did not like any of Harry's wives (there were three in all).

From a young age I can remember events such as Moseley's 'Blackshirts' marching along East Road at night, the triumphant return of Neville Chamberlain from Munich and my father writing to him with congratulations for averting a war in Europe. The reply from Downing Street was a prized possession for many years.

Of the death of George V, the abdication of Edward VIII and the succession of George VI, I was blissfully unaware. What I do remember was my father coming home with the evening paper and telling my mother that he thought war was inevitable. This must have been early in the summer of 1939.

If the weather was fine on a Sunday afternoon we would go by bus to Oxford Street and have tea at Lyon's Corner House, followed by a walk through Hyde Park. I saw soldiers digging trenches there in the summer of 1939. In reply to my question, my father said they were preparing for war. To me 'war' was just a word; its full implication was to be revealed to me over the coming weeks, months and years.

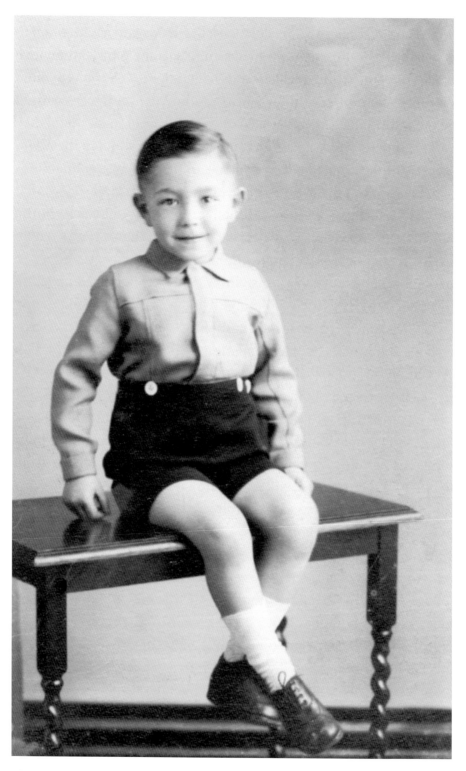

The author a few weeks before the outbreak of war.

Despite all the uncertainty in the summer of 1939, Betty and Lilly decided to go on holiday to the south of France. This was against advice from the Foreign Office and the family, but they were young and had never ventured further than Bournemouth or Brighton before. Aunt Jane was called in to look after Grandpa and my mother had to help out with the cooking as Jane's culinary skills went no further than successfully cremating water!

As the clouds gathered and Europe slid inevitably towards war, the aunts were still enjoying the sunshine in the south of France, oblivious to the warnings from the British Consul in Nice begging them to leave. I have learnt since that it was only when the handsome, bronzed young men were conscripted that they decided to return home.

1 September dawned and the future was quite clear; war was but a few days away. The great evacuation started on that day and on the Saturday I went with Uncle Harry and my grandfather in a taxi to, I believe, the headquarters of the Jewish Blind Society where the evacuation of their members was being coordinated. Apparently, the family had no idea of my grandfather's destination and it was some weeks later that we learned he was in Northampton, coincidentally about two miles from where I now live.

On Sunday 3 September it was our turn to be evacuated and my mother had decided that she would not let me go on my own, but would rather leave my father and the rest of the family in London. I had been attending nursery school since I was about three at Catherine Street School, where all the family had attended. Coaches were lined up in the school playground and our group consisted of children being accompanied by their mothers. We all carried our gas masks, but I cannot remember if we were made to wear labels. As we were saying our farewells to my father and Aunt Jane, who should arrive but Betty and Lilly. It was some time before we learnt of their horrendous journey from Nice to Calais as we just had time to say goodbye and board the coach. I do not think they ever realised how serious their plight would have been if they had been unable to get home. They were British and spoke not a word of French, which would have been bad enough, but being Jewish, they would have soon found themselves on a train to a concentration camp in Eastern Europe.

I believe we went to King's Cross Station and I have a vague memory of Neville Chamberlain's historic broadcast being relayed over the station tannoy. Certainly by the time we boarded the train we knew we were at war. At some point prior to 1 September we must have been issued with gas masks, but I cannot remember this. I do remember the younger children had 'Mickey Mouse' gas masks and for babies there was a device in which the baby was enclosed with a hand pump on the outside to ensure clean air inside. I have no idea how parents carried these around.

2

EVACUATION

I cannot recall much about the train journey but eventually we arrived at a town called Market Harborough in Leicestershire. By then it was dusk and a party of us boarded a bus which took us to the village of Dingley, where we assembled in the school before being billeted with local families. We were taken in by the Gotch family. The household consisted of Mr and Mrs Gotch, and a teenage son. They lived in a modern semi-detached house on the main road opposite the village school. We had a bedroom and otherwise lived with the family. Although the sanitation arrangements were far superior to East Road, the toilet was still in the garden.

Looking back, the one event that sticks in my mind is the Monday morning when we evacuee children all reported to the village school to be greeted by Miss Haslam, our nursery teacher from London, and our education continued seamlessly. Even with today's modern technology, I am not sure if the transition could have been achieved with greater efficiency.

The school comprised two rooms and all the children under eleven were taught in one class by Miss Haslam. The older pupils were in the other class, taught by the headmistress. This meant that different activities were going on at the same time in each class. There was

The author and his parents at Dingley, 1940.

no such thing as classroom assistants in those days but somehow I learned to read, write and do arithmetic. We used slates and chalk until we were proficient in writing and then progressed to paper and pencils. I was free of slate and chalk by my fifth birthday.

By this stage of the war there was talk of it being over by Christmas, just as they had said in 1914. But this was the 'Phoney War' – it was about to get infinitely worse.

However, just in case the Christmas forecast was a trifle optimistic, we were issued with identity cards and ration books. It was mandatory to carry your identity card and gas mask at all times. The ration book meant that you had to register with a grocer's for all general groceries and a butcher's for meat. Apart from being away from home, you could not use another shop for the rationed goods. If you went away from home you had to visit the food office and obtain emergency ration cards which could be used wherever you were staying. But in those cases you were not a 'regular customer' and your choices were severely limited. Although technically not allowed, there was an 'under the counter' favouritism culture in both the grocer's shop and the butcher's. If you were one of the privileged few, items in very short supply might find their way into your shopping basket.

They were happy days in Dingley; I loved my first taste of the countryside and walking in the woods with my school friends. But things were different for my mother. Firstly, she was not an easy person to get on with and it was not long before she fell out with Mrs Gotch, but probably her biggest problem was something the organisers of the evacuation had not foreseen – the cultural shock. My mother was a Londoner and to her London meant shops, cinemas, theatres and having the family around her. Suddenly, here she was living with a family of strangers with nothing in common and not a shop to be seen for miles except, of course, a Post Office in the village. Her solution was that every Saturday after lunch we would catch the bus into Market Harborough and here at least she could see a few shops. We normally visited the cinema, of which there were two,

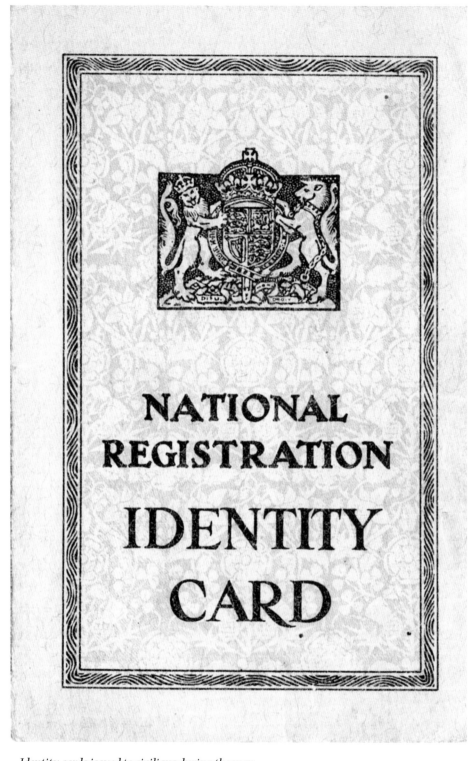

Identity cards issued to civilians during the war.

FOR OFFICIAL ENTRY ONLY (apart from Holder's Sign
MARKING OR ERASURE, IS PUNISHABLE F

NUMBER
RKGI 29.4

SURNAME
WOOD

CHRISTIAN NAMES (First only in full)
DEBORAH

CLASS CODE
A.

FULL POSTAL ADDRESS
Lewis Villa. Church Rd.
Basildon. Essex.

HOLDER'S SIGNATURE
D. Wood

CHANGES OF ADDRESS. No entry except by National
Registration Officer, to whom removal must be notified.

REMOVED TO (Full Postal Address)
8 Merron Road
SW2

The information recorded inside the author's mother's card.

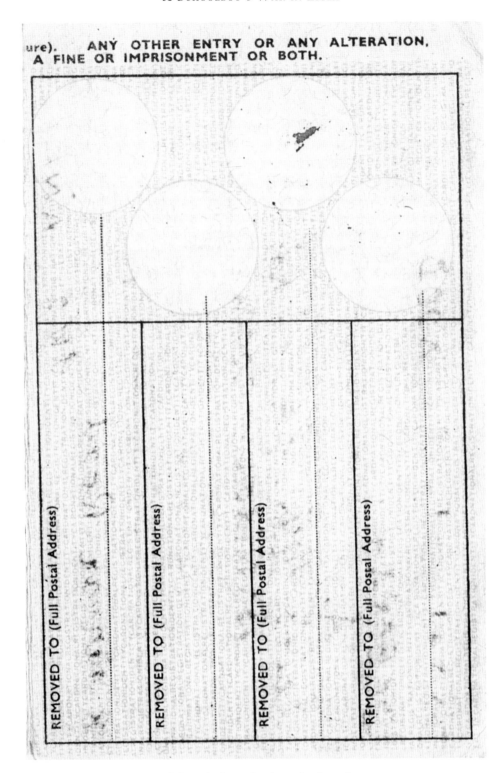

Further information recorded inside the author's mother's card.

NOTICE

FC 097074

1. Always carry your Identity Card. You must produce it on demand by a Police Officer in uniform or member of H.M. Armed Forces in uniform on duty.

2. **You are responsible for this Card, and must not part with it to any other person.** You must report at once to the local National Registration Office if it is lost, destroyed, damaged or defaced.

3. If you find a lost Identity Card or have in your possession a Card not belonging to yourself or anyone in your charge you must hand it in at once at a Police Station or National Registration Office.

4. Any breach of these requirements is an offence punishable by a fine or imprisonment or both.

FOR AUTHORISED ENDORSEMENTS ONLY

T 51/2878/1

The back cover of the identity card.

and follow that with tea and a cake before heading back on the last bus. I don't think those Saturday outings made up for what she was missing, but it had to suffice.

We did visit my grandfather in Northampton once, but the visit was never repeated; I have no idea what the reason was, it may have been because my mother did not get on with her father or, possibly, the fact that we got onto the wrong train on the return journey.

My father and the aunts corresponded regularly with us and at least they knew where we were, and Dad would occasionally send me drawings showing what he and the family were doing. I believe there was talk of a visit from my father, but the storm clouds were gathering in the Gotch household. The biggest problem must have been that my mother was bored. Mrs Gotch did the cooking and housework and my mother just sat around; she would not go out and enjoy the countryside because she didn't like it and made no effort. All she had ever done at home in London was cooking and housework and now Mrs Gotch was doing all that, something my mother obviously resented. I don't think it occurred to either of them to discuss the problem and possibly share the household tasks. Things were not helped by my mother suddenly being taken ill. I came home from school one day to be confronted by two very serious-looking doctors coming out of our bedroom. Of course I was too young to be told what was wrong, but sadly nothing further was done. This failure to act had almost catastrophic consequences some five years later.

The situation with the Gotch family must have reached breaking point when, by chance, my mother heard of an evacuee family that was returning to London. Within hours she had met with their landlady and arranged to take over the accommodation they were vacating. The landlady was a charming lady called Miss Vekary who lived in some splendour in a large cottage at the centre of the village, a large part of which was within Lord Beatty's estate – Dingley Hall. We had our own kitchen-cum-living room and a beautiful bedroom in the main part of the house. Water had to be drawn from the village pump opposite and the toilet was still at the bottom of the garden.

There was an inside toilet but I was only allowed to use it if I was ill. Drawing water from the pump must have been something my mother could live with in order to have her own kitchen and a degree of independence. Also, this meant that my father could visit for the odd weekend, although train travel at that time was fraught with delays.

Miss Vekary was what might be described as an eccentric spinster; every village seems to have had one in those days. For example, on hunt days she would secure the gates to her drive and stand in front of them in defiance of the huntsmen. She was a pillar of the church and insisted on taking me to Sunday morning services. One advantage to me was that on alternate Sundays the service was held at Brampton Ash Church, a few miles from Dingley, which meant I got to travel in her Morris Eight car. My mother used to avoid the services but was somehow recruited onto the flower arranging rota. I don't think she ever told the family about that. My mother was not artistic in the least, so I cannot imagine the results of her endeavours.

My time at Dingley living in Miss Vekary's house was one of the happiest periods of my early childhood, but like all things in life, nothing lasts forever and things were about to change.

Christmas 1939 was something I shall always remember. Dad and Auntie Bet had come to visit and in the evening of Christmas Day we were invited to join Miss Vekary and her guests. I had never been in her lounge before and it was a magnificent room, but the surprise for me was the tree. Being Jewish, we did not celebrate Christmas so I knew nothing of trees, lights, decorations and Christmas presents. Suddenly I was plunged into what, to me, was a wonderful fairyland. Added to that, there were presents under the tree bearing my name. I became a firm fan of Father Christmas from that day. Sadly, all too soon Christmas was over and it was time for Dad and Auntie Bet to return to London.

In those days, New Year was just a date – there was no day off in England – but January 1940 ushered in an extremely cold spell which lasted many weeks. Dingley was virtually cut off but my mother refused to accept that the isolation applied to her as well as the rest of the village. So, Saturday afternoon saw us standing at the bus stop waiting for a non-existent bus to take us into Market Harborough. We waited and waited and we were eventually rewarded by a large shooting brake from Dingley Hall pulling up and giving us a lift. I have racked my memory but cannot remember how we got back in the evening, we may have been picked up again by the estate vehicle. What I do remember is that one of the two cinemas was closed and we had to see a film that my mother didn't want to see. That incident was typical of her forceful character; if she wanted something then nothing would stand in her way.

Whilst my mother and I were enjoying a rather quiet start to 1940, a man was about to enter the life of our family whose presence was to influence all of us for many years to come. JL, as I shall call him, owned a fleet of black cabs which were based at a garage in Kennington, South London. He was in the habit of visiting the East End in his car, indulging in what we now call 'curb crawling' and trying to pick up factory girls. This had nothing to do with prostitution; it was just picking up girls for a drink and possibly a meal or perhaps a visit to a dance. This practice was quite common and I met a man many years later who actually bought an American left-hand drive car for the purpose. JL made a date with one of Auntie Bet's friends but at the last minute she got cold feet. Auntie Bet was game for anything and went in her place. What happened on that first date is unknown, but JL suddenly became very involved in the life of our family. He owned a lot of property in South London and was actually buying anything that came up for sale whilst most people were fleeing the capital. He also owned a large number of houses and land in Basildon, Essex. In the early part of the century, the government offered land for sale at an almost giveaway price. I believe the object was to encourage people to become self-sufficient and thus relieve the unemployment situation. The land was known as the 'champagne lands' because prospective buyers were entertained with free champagne lunches. Some of the land was sold for one guinea (£1.05) an acre. By today's standards, JL would have been a multi-millionaire.

The first my mother and I knew of JL was when we received a letter from my father informing us that that the whole family had left East Road and moved to Hayter Road, Brixton, South London. They had rented a large house owned by JL and this was intended to be the family home for the duration of the war.

My mother, being the eldest sibling, was not happy that things were happening in London regarding the family without her involvement, so she decided that an urgent visit to London was called for. The London that we encountered was rather different from what we had left in September 1939. Sandbags were everywhere and a large number of taxis were towing fire tenders. Such cars as there were had their headlights covered so that only a sliver of light showed and many had the front wings painted white to make them visible to pedestrians in the blackout. Many pedestrians were killed by not seeing approaching vehicles. Overhead in the sky were barrage balloons, which were large, cigar-shaped objects anchored to the ground by steel cables. Their purpose was to create a dense barrier of wires which it was hoped would slice through the wings of enemy aircraft. How our own planes were expected to fare I have no idea. There were women in khaki and we had seen the birth of the Auxiliary Territorial Service (ATS), later to become the Women's Royal Army Corps (WRAC). Another phenomenon was cars with large gas tanks on their roofs in an attempt to get round petrol rationing. They ran on coal-gas and the tanks themselves were made of canvas. Presumably the safety aspect was the reason for their demise. I have often wondered if the technology employed in constructing those tanks was the forerunner of today's vehicles being fuelled by LPG.

This first visit to Brixton must have been around the spring of 1940 and my mother was not happy with what she found at Hayter Road. The first crisis was the discovery that the aunts had taken the best bedroom for themselves and furnished it with Mum and Dad's bedroom suite. My father, being no match for the aunts, had been consigned to a bedroom on the second floor with nothing more than a bed. Similarly, all our other furniture had been taken over by the aunts and, as far as I remember, their only contribution was a piano. Apparently Grandpa had bought the piano when the children were young, probably as a status symbol, but in the hope that one of his children might be musical. Sadly this was not the case; my mother thought she could play but what she actually did was to hit a few keys and sing a loud, tuneless melody to drown out the sound of the piano. Times were hard in the thirties and my parents must have worked and saved hard to acquire a nice home. My mother's indignation was understandable. Auntie Lill was back in business as a dressmaker and she had a brass plate outside the house which read: 'Lillian, high class dressmaker'.

My grandfather had mysteriously returned from Northampton. No reason was ever given for this but his host family had probably found coping with a blind and infirm guest too much for them.

Auntie Bet had left the hat factory where she had worked for some time as, in common with most of the hat industry, operations were being moved to Luton. She was now working for JL in the office of his garage. My father had moved premises and now had a workshop in Gosset Street, Bethnal Green, and was busily engaged manufacturing beds for the Army. Uncle Jack had enlisted in the RAF despite having served in France in the First World War

Our visit to Brixton only lasted a few days and we returned to Dingley, but the visit had unsettled my mother. She missed London and the family. Also, I believe there was a degree of moral blackmail over the care of my grandfather. Things did not seem too bad in London, which was leading to a gradual drift back by many evacuee families.

3

BACK TO LONDON

By around June 1940 the lure of London proved too great and we said farewell to Miss Vekary and Dingley amid tears and promises to keep in touch. We settled in at Hayter Road and my new school was opposite our house. It was called Sudbourne Road School because it was situated between the two roads. JL had converted what must have been an indoor coal store into a shelter by reinforcing the ceiling with large wooden beams from floor to ceiling. Being inside the house, it was quite comfortable; we had electric light but had to sleep on the floor. But it was far superior to the outdoor shelters installed by the government.

Our return to London coincided with the commencement of the Battle of Britain. The Phoney War was over and we suddenly found ourselves under attack night and day. We spent a lot of time in our shelter and to a five-year-old this was quite exciting, but it must have taken its toll on the grown-ups. We were issued with rolls of brown sticky paper which we attached to all the windows in a criss-cross pattern, the object being to prevent flying glass. The blackout was very strictly enforced; no lights were allowed to be seen from outside after lighting up time. Windows were fitted with heavy blackout curtains and if so much as a chink of light was observed by the wardens on patrol, they could be heard shouting 'Put that light out!', usually accompanied by a furious banging on the door. Cases of persistent offending resulted in court appearances and a fine.

Soon after our arrival in Brixton, JL invited us to visit his house in Basildon and this was quite an adventure. He picked us up in his car, a mid-1930s Austin 10 and Auntie Lill stayed behind to look after Grandfather, leaving my mother and father, Auntie Bet and I to have a weekend away from London.

The journey itself was not without incident; Basildon being quite close to the Essex coast was in a restricted area and we were stopped several times at road blocks and had to produce identity cards. JL also had a pass allowing him into the area.

I am not sure what we expected at Basildon, but it must have been quite a shock to the grown-ups, as JL seemed to own half the village. His own house, Joetta, was part of a large poultry farm which was run by a Mr Bland, who occupied an adjoining house called Roseddie. JL named all his houses after family members; he also always named one of his horses Hetty, after his wife. Although my time in Dingley had given me an understanding of the countryside, Basildon was something else. JL's 'estate' comprised not only the poultry farm but acres of grazing land with six or seven horses, stables, a large pigeon loft and the biggest surprise of all, a swimming pool. The inside of the house also had quite a few surprises. JL was gadget mad and had the means to indulge his passion. I think some of his so-called labour saving devices were things my parents had never encountered. As far as I recall there was no gas in the house and cooking and heating was either by electricity or coal. I don't think my mother had ever used an electric cooker or refrigerator and as for heating the water by immersion heater, this must have been quite beyond her.

But the best was yet to come. There was one huge room in the house and on that Saturday evening it became a cinema. The curtains were closed, a screen erected and we were entertained to a number of films of JL's family weddings. Being larger than life, JL didn't use 8mm or 9.5mm, which was the format of most amateurs, he used 16mm

The author and Doris outside the buildings in Thrawl Street, 1940.

which produced near professional quality. It didn't matter that there was no sound and we didn't know the people involved, this was luxury. In the same room was a pinball machine that I had endless fun playing on.

Another surprise awaited me in the hall. By pulling a chain suspended from the ceiling, a trap door came down exposing a sliding staircase. This led to the first floor, which contained JL's bedroom and a bathroom.

I was introduced to horse riding on Sunday morning and that experience was probably the start of my lifelong affection for horses. As I remember I did more falling off than riding, but it was fun. We did actually get my mother on a horse but it was not an experience that she chose to repeat.

All too soon it was time to return to the real world in London. It was school holidays for me and during that period my school became a depot for the fire service and we were allocated places in various other schools from September.

Hitler had now conquered most of Western Europe and was free to concentrate his attention on England, heralding the real start of the Battle of Britain. The first air raid on London was on the night of 23 August 1940 and, following a reprisal raid on Berlin, the 'Blitz' was born. At my young age I had trouble with an obviously German word being used to describe the bombing. Surely that was unpatriotic? Although I was too young to know that word, Blitz, of course, was short for *blitzkrieg*, which was the term used to describe the rapid advance across both Eastern and Western Europe by the German Army. The literal translation of *blitzkrieg* is 'lightning storm'. But why use a German word? I never found an answer to that question, but it did describe what London and other major towns were suffering. My mother was of an age to remember the Zeppelin raids of the First World War, so she was no stranger to attacks from the air, but she had to admit there was no comparison to the type of attack to which we were now subjected. Almost every evening the air raid sirens would sound and we would retreat to our shelter where we would stay until the welcome sound of the all-clear. Then the first task of the grown-ups was to check the house for damage, especially broken windows. We were not immune during the day either, and daytime raids were becoming common. At the age of five I knew no fear and I would often slip out of the shelter during the daylight raids and stand outside the house wearing my tin hat, gas mask and carrying my wooden rifle. My father had to have serious words with me over this. He told me that the firemen and air raid wardens across the road had complained that I was doing their job.

After all these years it is difficult to describe the bombing. It is often equated to a thunder storm, but it was much worse and far more terrifying. The siren was quite frightening with its continuous, monotone howling and yes, you heard the bombers overhead but you didn't really know where they were; the engine noise could be deceiving and even if you saw them caught in the searchlight beams it was still difficult to determine their location. It was said that the bomb destined for you made no noise, and if you heard the whistle of the bomb it would fall elsewhere. This was of very little comfort as we cowered in our shelters. The explosion when it came was deafening, often followed by an aftershock. Then came the sound of falling masonry and quite often the sounds of gas mains exploding. It wasn't just one explosion, there would be a whole series of them as something like 100 bombers could be overhead. The bomb explosions were accompanied by the sound of the anti-aircraft guns and their exploding shells. Then there were the incendiary bombs, usually dropped in 'sticks' and sometimes causing more damage than the high explosive bombs. Some of the high explosive bombs were equipped with a device which made a high-pitched whistle as they approached the ground and that was very frightening. There were Stuka dive bombers, also fitted with a high pitched sound but I cannot ever recall those; I know they were very prominent in the battle for France. The next sounds were the bells of the fire engines and ambulances racing to the scene of the latest devastation. All emergency vehicles had bells in those days. All this didn't mean too much to me, but I often wonder how the adults coped, bearing in mind that they still had to face the horror of what would greet them when the all-clear sounded. Was the house still intact? Were our neighbours safe? Could they get to work in the morning? Servicemen on leave would remark that the civilian population was going through more terror than they were and they couldn't wait to get back to camp.

One other aspect of the bombing was blast damage. This was totally silent and the result of the force of the explosion sucking out the surrounding air. The awful consequence of this was that people would be found dead without a mark on them. They had literally had the air sucked out of their bodies. For some reason this type of death was seen as more tragic than someone dying from visible injuries.

One highlight at that time, of which I still have fond memories, was when my father would come up to the bedroom when he returned from work and before the sirens to recount stories of his experiences in India during the First World War. He served the whole war in the Khyber Pass region, which was as savage then as it is now, the only difference being that they now have more sophisticated weapons. His job was in signals and in those days signalling was by heliographs, which were giant mirrors used to transmit messages by Morse code. As I understood it, the area was extremely violent and although he never fired a shot in anger, many of his colleagues were killed or tortured. Sadly, nearly 100 years later things have not changed very much. A lot of his stories seemed to involve falling into trenches whilst returning to barracks and it was many years before I realised that these situations were not, as he led me to believe, the result of drinking too much tea!

By the beginning of September the air raids had become severe. On one particular Saturday evening I was standing in our back garden with my father and the sky was red with the flames from the Surrey Commercial Docks, which had been one of the German targets that night. I think this was the turning point for my parents and by the following weekend we were on our way back to Basildon. By this time JL had changed his car and was now driving a rather luxurious 1939 Austin 6, which he kept for the rest of his life. It was arranged that my mother, Auntie Lill and I would stay in JL's house and my father would come down with JL each weekend. Auntie Lill could run her dressmaking business from there by commuting to London once a week to see her customers and purchase materials, etc. Because we were technically at war with Russia and my grandfather had never become a British citizen, he was classified as an 'enemy alien' and needed permission to move to Basildon, so he stayed in London with my father and Auntie Bet whilst they waited for the permit. I have no idea how he coped during the day whilst they were both at work.

4

JOETTA

On our first visit to Joetta there had been about twelve large chicken houses, each of which must have contained at least 100 chickens. The whole operation was run by Mr Bland, in partnership with JL. However, when we arrived on our second visit most of these buildings had gone and the chicken stock was much reduced. I never found out the reason for this but it was probably yet another of JL's Machiavellian manoeuvrings, of which there were many. I don't think there was much love lost between them; possibly a degree of anti-Semitism existed. Mrs Bland did not mix with us and their son, Derek, who was slightly younger than me, was not encouraged to socialise. We were seen as part of JL's family, although my mother was always at pains to explain that this was not the case. Racism in the form of anti-Semitism was around then in quite a big way.

The Basildon that was to be my home for the next ten years was nothing like the town of today. Basically it consisted of one main road, Church Road, where we lived. The boundaries were rather difficult to define but it was probably from where Church Road met Bull Road at a 'T' junction, to the other end of Church Road where it met Rectory Road at another 'T' junction. Between those two junctions the 'shanty town' of Basildon grew in all directions. Most of the 'roads' were nothing more than footpaths, usually running between fields. The only other surfaced roads were Gordon Road and Fairview Road, both of which had been developed by the construction of small, wooden bungalows bearing such names as 'Dunroamin' or 'Alfedith'. There were no house numbers. Amenities were few. There was a small Post Office and stores at the junction with Gordon Road and further towards the church was Basildon Stores, owned by JL and leased to Mrs Pulford. Most of the houses were self-built and very primitive. The story went that most were built as weekend retreats by the owners, who brought the materials on the train from the East End on each visit. That may or may not be true but several of the bungalows close to the railway seemed to have a large number of railway sleepers in their construction. The nearest railway station was at Pitsea, about three miles away, served by a bus service four or five times a day. Suddenly these weekend retreats became homes to the owners.

Pitsea was also the destination for any serious shopping. There wasn't much at Pitsea, but it had the Broadway cinema, two banks (Lloyds and Midland), a police station and a doctor's surgery. There was also the Railway Hotel and, on Broadway Parade, a ladies hairdressers. Next door to the hairdressers was Mence Smith. Now that was a quite unique shop; it was known as the 'oil shop' because it sold paraffin for the lamps and heaters but it was much, much more. They sold just about everything in Mence Smith, from household to gardening products and if they didn't stock what you were looking for, it probably didn't exist. But above all there was the smell, a combination of paraffin, candles, moth balls and fertiliser. I have never known another shop like it for real atmosphere. Pitsea also had a market, mainly under cover, which operated on Wednesdays and Saturdays. Apart from the cinema, I don't think there was any other entertainment.

Beyond the railway station there was Pitsea Creek, a tributary of the River Thames. Some of the children used to swim there, but it was very dangerous as the incoming tide could be quite fast-flowing. A few local children drowned there.

Although a country area away from London, Basildon was not a designated evacuation area. This meant that most of the incomers from London had some connection with the village, either by having a weekend retreat or possibly relatives already resident. Thus, there was not a huge influx of evacuees to be accommodated in both homes and schools. In many ways this made it more difficult for us to be assimilated into the local population. We were outsiders and treated as such. When Dad asked one of the locals about this attitude, he replied that it took about ten years to be accepted in a countryside community.

There were a number of houses which were probably Victorian or Edwardian and the church was reputedly thirteenth century. Adjoining the church was Manor Farm, run by the Stevens family, who had, I believe, farmed in Basildon for several generations. Their house was rather grand and whilst their daughter, Joyce, was in my class, there was no socialising. The farm supplied milk to most of us and it was delivered by Mr Challis in wide-necked bottles with a cardboard lid, which was difficult to open without splashing milk in all directions. The Challis family had a son in the Army who was a prisoner of war. His fiancée, Jean, was in the ATS and used to visit the Challis family every weekend; they were married as soon as he got home after the war.

A number of people lived in converted railway carriages and even small huts constructed of corrugated iron. These places had no facilities whatsoever; sanitation was an earth closet at the bottom of the garden, fresh water was obtained either by collecting rainwater or renting a key from the Essex Water Company, which gave access to a brick cupboard containing a tap. There was only one such tap, and it was situated close to the village hall and Post Office. Distance must have been a real problem for some residents who lived up to half a mile away. Cooking and lighting were by paraffin appliances and if you owned a radio it was powered by an accumulator (similar to a car battery) which had to be taken to the local shop periodically to be recharged. Bathing was by way of a tin bath, with water heated on the paraffin stove. The whole family would use the same water, which then had to be emptied bucket by bucket. I don't think a lot of bathing took place.

For us living in Joetta, life was rather less primitive. We had mains water and electricity, gas was available but not used and drainage was by a cesspit which had to be emptied periodically by a contractor. It seems ironic looking back that even the swimming pool was powered by electricity and yet no more than 500yds away, families were existing with oil lamps and paraffin cookers. Viewed from the outside, and in contrast to the interior, Joetta was a rather ugly chalet bungalow built to a basic design with rooms on each corner. At the front there was a bedroom on one side and a large dining room on the other which also contained a 'put-u-up' – our bedroom for the coming months. At the back was another bedroom with a toilet next to it, while the kitchen and living room occupied the other corner. In addition there was the first floor containing JL's bedroom and the bathroom.

JL always had men working on various projects and his main workforce comprised Billy Austin and Percy Pym. Billy was a general builder who today would be called a 'bodger'. He went everywhere on a bicycle so his tools were few. He suffered badly from rheumatism and some days could hardly walk. Billy eventually bought one of JL's horses and went around in a cart. This might have improved his mobility but it did nothing to improve his building skills.

Percy Pym was a carpenter who worked in London during the week and did jobs for JL on Sunday mornings. He was not only an excellent craftsman but also a very pleasant man who had been a widower for some years. He lived at the top of Church Road and took pride in showing visitors his pre-war Ford car jacked up on blocks in his garage. This was what happened to a lot of cars once petrol became almost unobtainable.

Another example of JL's mania for technology was the air raid shelter. Since before the war the government had been installing

Anderson shelters. These consisted of a tunnel-like structure made of corrugated steel set in a concrete base and covered with earth. The front was open, although there was a separate metal sheet which could be placed over the entrance. However, these were hardly ever used and this sometimes had fatal consequences, as I shall recount later. JL's version was rather more elaborate and it was large enough to accommodate at least twelve people. The Bland family shared the shelter with us. It had two hermetically sealed doors at the foot of a flight of stairs, presumably a defence against a gas attack, with an entrance lobby between the doors. There were bunks, electric lights and an escape hatch at the far end. The only flaw was that fresh air was fed in by way of tubes set in the roof. Unfortunately, these also let in the rain. On my first stay in the shelter, I awoke during the night soaking wet and my mother decided she would rather risk the bombing than me catching pneumonia. As far as I remember, the shelter was never used by us again.

I spent the first few weeks exploring Joetta's grounds. Despite the removal of many of the buildings, it still comprised a rather large poultry farm run by Mr Bland, a somewhat neglected orchard, acres of grazing for the horses and, of course, the pigeon loft and the swimming pool. Mr Bland had a young man working for him called Don who was waiting to be called up. Don showed me the various aspects of the farm, including a rather gruesome ritual on Fridays which involved killing a number of chickens. These were birds whose egg laying days were over and some of them were for JL, who insisted that his chickens were killed in the traditional Jewish way, which involved having their throats cut and being hung up by the legs until all the blood drained from their bodies. The remainder were killed by having their necks wrung. This procedure was seen as part of the everyday running of a poultry farm; chickens were not bred as pets, they existed to feed us, firstly with eggs and secondly with meat. The family never understood why JL insisted on his birds being killed in this manner as he was singularly ignorant about all other aspects of the Jewish religion. It was assumed that it was necessary for the recipients of the dead chickens, whoever they were. Don was eventually called up to join the Army and I was sad to see him go. We never heard of him again.

Whilst I was exploring the grounds I discovered a rather ancient Bullnose Morris Cowley in one of the stables. I have often read accounts of these old vehicles being discovered all covered in straw and this was exactly what I found. The car must have been from the late 1920s; it was a cream-coloured, two-seater coupé with a 'dickie' seat at the rear which was open to the elements when in use. The Bullnose was made of gleaming brass and the whole vehicle looked very grand. The car actually belonged to Mr Bland and he might have been hiding it from JL. Of course, he reckoned without me telling everyone of my find and it wasn't long before this lovely old car was being towed out of the stable by one of the horses and consigned to a field where it stood for as long as I can remember. Such were the machinations of JL's devious mind.

In the course of my wanderings around the farm I was spotted by the dreaded School Board man. He was a very familiar figure in those days and his job seemed to involve travelling round the area on his bicycle looking for children playing truant. Both children and parents went in fear of him. I was taken back to the house and it was my mother, rather than me, who was in trouble. Suitably chastised, she marched me off to the local school in Vange the following morning. The headmaster was a Geordie named John Scorer and he was to have a very important influence on my future education.

Vange Primary School was built in the late nineteenth-century when education was rather less extensive than some forty years later. The main brick-built building comprised two classrooms, the headmaster's study, kitchens and an enormous school hall with a large stage, totally out of proportion to the number of intended pupils. A later addition was a separate wooden building which housed a staffroom and four more classrooms to accommodate the older pupils.

As a five-year-old I missed the youngest class and started in Miss O'Shea's class. I cannot remember much about her except that she was a fiery redhead who always seemed to be threatening to go home. She kept her coat handy and at least once a day put it on and had the door open before the class begged her to stay. I have to admit that I was not amongst the majority begging her to stay. I did not remain in Miss O'Shea's class for more than one term as I was able to read and write. I was ahead of the most of the other pupils who were still using slates and chalk.

After Miss O'Shea, I moved into the other building and my teacher was Miss Coleman, a lovely lady who was engaged to another teacher, Mr Pickering, who was in the Army. He used to visit us when on leave and tell us stories of his wartime experiences. They married after the war and he eventually succeeded Mr Scorer as headmaster.

After Miss Coleman, my next teacher was Mrs Scorer, wife of the headmaster. She had a vastly different style of teaching to Miss Coleman and I did not really enjoy my year in her class, particularly her attempts at teaching me to sing.

My next teacher was Miss Marvin, who must have been close to retirement. She was a gentle, encouraging teacher who clearly loved her job and had time for all her pupils. A rare breed even in those days.

I did not stay very long in Miss Marvin's class as Mr Scorer was in the habit of picking the brightest pupils to move straight into the top class, with a view to being coached for the eleven-plus. I therefore found myself in the top class with Miss Webb. She was no stranger to me as she lived quite close to us and would cycle past our house every day. Doris Webb was very young, not long out of teacher training college and liked by all the pupils. Not only did she teach the usual subjects, but also PE and dancing. Strangely, she did not teach the dances of the time but such things as the polka and the valeta. Towards the end of term we did get a few lessons in the waltz, but it would have been nice to have had more of that and less old time. I think Doris Webb was the most popular teacher in the school and

ESSEX EDUCATION COMMITTEE.

VANGE COUNCIL MIXED SCHOOL.

REPORT *for* Summer Term, 19 45

Name David Wood Age 10 yrs 9 mths

Class 1 No. in Class 51 Average Age in Class 10 yrs 10 mths

Max.	Examination. Score.	Position.		Remarks on work during Term.
			Reading	V. Good
			Language (Oral)	Good.
			„ (Written)	Good, but untidy.
			Spelling	Good.
			Literature	V. Good.
			Handwriting	Irregular.
			Arithmetic (Mental)	Good
			„ (Written)	Good.
			Geography	V. Good ⎱ Shows keen interest
			History	V. Good ⎰ and answers well.
			Art	Fair
			Handwork	
			Nature	Good.
			Physical Training	Good.
			Music	J

Attendance Good until latterly. Punctuality V. Good.

Conduct Excellent.

General Remarks David will go far, because he takes his work seriously & always does his best! Excellent progress. Should do well. Best wishes.

S. M. Webb. Class Master. Jascon. Head Master.
Mistress. Mistress.

P. & T. LTD.

I certify that I have received the School Report.

Signature of Parent or Guardian

This slip should be signed by the Parent (or Guardian) of the Scholar and returned to the Head Teacher as soon as possible.

The author's school report from 1945.

had an inspiring way of teaching. She was, however, quite a tough disciplinarian, but very fair in dishing out punishment.

Mr Scorer used to teach singing and I think this was one subject where I made him despair. My voice was terrible, in fact it still is, and he described it as similar to breaking coke. Quite often in the middle of singing he would shout out 'Shut up Wood!' and in the end I didn't bother to go to his singing classes. He was probably relieved as nothing was ever said about my absence.

Every morning at about 10 a.m. we were served with milk. This came in the same third-of-a-pint bottle with the wide neck and cardboard cap that we had at home, and was the cause of many accidents in the class. If you pressed too hard the top would get pushed into the bottle, causing a large splash of milk to go over yourself and any books on the desk. On reflection, I used to dread those milk bottles and tried to avoid drinking milk at the morning break.

I have never forgotten the school dinners, which were some of the best I ever tasted. The kitchen was run by Mrs Bates and her shepherd's pie was to die for. For many of the children this was probably their only meal as there was a great deal of abject poverty; many children only possessed the clothes they stood up in. Quite often, children would be absent because their clothes were in the wash or their boots or shoes were being mended. Even finding money for the school dinners (2d per week) must have been a struggle. I cannot ever recall such problems in our house, we were not well off but money was never tight and we certainly did not go short of food. Much of the credit for that must be down to my mother, who managed the family finances with a rod of iron. She always ensured that my father and I were smartly dressed when we went out and she never left the house unless she wore a hat and matching gloves. This was the case even if she was only going to the local shop. But not all wives and mothers were good managers and many had nothing but their Army marriage allowance plus anything their husbands sent in addition. Many husbands would rather spend their meagre pay in the pub with very little thought for their families struggling at home.

Rationing continued to bite, with only the basics remaining on the shelves. As always, the British were up to the challenge and such strange concoctions as the 'Woolton pie' were promoted by the government. The recipe was named after the wife of the then Food Minister, Lord Woolton, whose wife had reputedly come up with a series of wartime recipes to help housewives cope with the food shortages, particularly of meat. It was called the 'meatless pie' and, as I remember, comprised potatoes, carrots and any available root vegetables with a piecrust on top. I don't remember my mother ever making this pie but if you went to a British Restaurant, a government-sponsored series of eating places, it was always at the top of the menu. Sometimes it was the only item on the menu.

Other ways to get round the seasonal shortages of produce was to preserve them. Even with your own chickens there were periods when egg production would fall off, so at times of high egg production we preserved the eggs in 'Isinglass', which was a semi-transparent jelly-like substance which was placed in a bucket; the eggs would be added and a lid placed over the top. Apparently the eggs would last indefinitely in this solution and they were quite palatable, although they did not taste all that nice if boiled. It was certainly a preferable alternative to the dried egg powder which was coming from America.

Sadly as the war progressed many young wives were receiving the dreaded telegram from the War Office announcing that their loved one was either dead or missing. I don't think a week went by in school without one of the children being bereaved. But this was war and death was with us all the time.

By September 1940 the Battle of Britain was at its most severe. We were situated between fighter stations at Hornchurch, North Weald and Debden. Duxford was also not far away. This meant that we saw a lot of fighter activity and we witnessed dogfights several times each day. Dogfights were one-to-one battles between two fighter planes, with each pilot using his aerobatic skills to manoeuvre his plane into the right position to deliver the fatal shot that would either destroy the enemy aircraft or incapacitate the pilot. The survival chances for the pilot once the plane was hit were not very high; he needed to ditch the canopy and deploy his parachute, otherwise he would go down with his plane. A lot of pilots perished due to the canopy sticking or the plane being on fire. Cheers would go up if a German fighter was hit and quite a few crashed fairly close to us. Local farmers would be waiting with shotguns or pitchforks for any pilots fortunate enough to parachute to safety. Often they did not know the nationality of the survivor until he landed and even then there was confusion if the parachutist was Polish, Czech or French. If a plane came down close to us, we kids would rush off hunting for souvenirs but they were usually too far away for our little legs. We had no fear of the danger of approaching a damaged aircraft that could burst into flames at any moment. Victorious pilots would do a victory roll, sometimes coming so low that we could wave to them. There were always aircraft in the sky and we learnt to identify them not only visually but by engine noise. This was particularly so at night when it was possible to identify enemy bombers by the sound from the engine. They were either 'one of ours' or 'one of theirs'.

Basildon, being in a direct line from the coast to London and quite close to the Thames, saw a lot of aerial activity. However, most of the enemy bombers were on their way to or from a raid and in those early days we suffered hardly any bomb damage. However, one Saturday night in September 1940 an attack was made on a small factory in the village. The attack may have been deliberate or the bomb aimer might have mistaken his target. This factory produced electric cables which must have been vital to the war effort. They failed to make a direct hit on the factory, but severely damaged the owner's house which was next door. Also, two houses about half a mile from the factory and very close to us were destroyed, but I do not recall any casualties. The factory was working as usual on Monday morning, but the owner now found himself living in a bungalow having lost the whole first floor of his house.

We settled into a comfortable routine with me at school, Auntie Lill working on her dressmaking and my mother in charge of housework and cooking. Rationing was gradually becoming part of our lives but I do not recall any food shortages for us at that time. We were well-supplied with eggs and poultry and my mother seemed to manage very well on the food allowances. But the war was only just a year old and it must have been easy to get complacent. My father would come with JL every Saturday and keep us up to date on events in London. Each week there would be news of yet another landmark destroyed and it must have been hard for the adults to maintain optimism. The newspapers didn't help much as they had very little to report apart from depressing war news.

We had no shortage of visitors as the aunts had a wealth of friends, mostly girlfriends, who would descend on us for the weekend. The sleeping arrangements were a bit of a mystery because there were more women than beds. Some of them seemed to sleep head-to-toe and going into their bedrooms you were never quite certain whose heads matched whose feet. Whether JL had a hand in easing the overnight congestion I had no idea. From what I learned of him in later years, the answer was probably yes.

My mother was not really cut out to be a country wife but she did try. One day she decided to feed some stale bread to the horses in the nearest paddock. One horse was particularly friendly; too friendly in fact. She was a very large Russian mare with the most enormous pink eyes and was the first horse that I ever rode. Mum threw her some crusts but she wanted more and kept coming towards us. We backed up to the gate and still she kept coming. Mum's courage totally failed her and she threw the basket at the horse, dragged me through the gate and fled back to the house. We never saw the basket again.

On another occasion Mum woke me up one morning and I was taken out to one of the paddocks where a mare had given birth to a beautiful foal overnight. By the time I returned from school that afternoon the foal was walking about on long, spindly legs. I tried to equate this to babies but I could not understand how a newborn animal could be walking around less than twenty-four hours after being born. Clearly I had a lot to learn about country life.

One mystery regarding JL was the whereabouts of his family. Surely it would have made sense for the family to leave Streatham and move to Basildon? The truth was that his family disliked both him and his place in Basildon. Their name for it was 'Pigshit Farm', which was rather odd because there were no pigs to be seen and it was hardly an appropriate name for a Jewish-owned property! They had actually decamped to Ampthill in Bedfordshire and it was not until after the war that we made their acquaintance.

My father's mother lived in Clapham, only a few minutes from our house in Brixton, and I remember her as a little old lady who must have been in her early eighties at the beginning of the war. One day we received a rather puzzling letter from her, stating that she hoped that the damage to our house wasn't too bad. This rang alarm bells, but it was decided to wait until the weekend to get more news. As soon as my father got out of the car on Saturday, my mother knew something serious had happened. The clue was that he was wearing a new suit. Dad and new suits did not go together. He had to be physically dragged into a shop to buy new clothes so something must have occurred. He had gone to work on 4 October 1940, leaving Aunt Bet to clear out the attic rooms, which presented a fire hazard, and start closing the house up. They planned to live entirely on the ground floor, as it was seen to be the safest part of the house. My grandfather was in his usual place by the fire in the rear living room. After lunch, Auntie Bet had had enough of household chores and went to the office, leaving my grandfather in his usual position. During the afternoon, the house sustained a direct hit and was totally destroyed, apart from the corner where Grandpa was sitting and the indoor shelter. He always wore a trilby hat in the house and that probably saved him from being seriously injured by falling plaster. Obviously he had no idea what had happened but he was aware of a cold draught and could hear voices calling. He got out of his chair and immediately fell over some rubble. He then called out that he was blind and within a short time he was rescued and taken to a rest centre at Stockwell, about a mile away. He didn't have a scratch on him. Auntie Bet came home soon after and was taken to the rest centre to be reunited with Grandpa. When my father arrived home the road was barricaded and the warden in charge told him that our house and the one next door had gone. He said a blind man had been rescued but a lady who had been taking a bath had been killed. This was devastating news and my father went to the rest centre in a daze, convinced that Auntie Bet was dead. Imagine his relief when he found her fit and well with Grandpa. That was probably one of the few occasions when my father was reduced to tears. The casualty had been the lady who lived next door. Years later, whilst doing my National Service, I was in a hotel in Ventnor chatting to a friend of the landlady who turned out to be the daughter of the lady killed that day.

It was a wartime policy for the government to give an immediate emergency cash grant to anyone who had lost all their possessions in the bombing. They offered my father 30s to purchase new clothes. At first my father rather indignantly refused their offer, but after a night's sleep accepted the money. Hence the new suit. Believe it or not, a new suit could be purchased for that amount in those days. We now had no house, no furniture and only the clothes we had with us. There was a government compensation scheme but that took time to process.

By coincidence, Grandma had decided to leave London and move to Noak Hill, a small village on the outskirts of Romford and just a few miles from us in Basildon. Her origins were in Essex and her cousin's family, the Quilters, had quite a large farm there. Grandma's cousin, Jim, had handed the farm over to his son, Percy, and lived in a small bungalow across the road from the farm. Grandma would be his housekeeper and also look after a mysterious lady known as Miss Kate. We never found out who she was or where she figured in the domestic arrangements, but she was an invalid when we met her and died shortly after Grandma's arrival. Having left London, there remained the problem of Grandma's furniture, which she immediately offered to my parents. JL arranged for one of the barns to be emptied and Grandma's possessions were collected from Clapham and stored until we had our own house. Grandma's plan, not shared by my mother, was that she would come to live with us after the war. By chance, we had our own house sooner than expected.

The war continued and towards the end of 1940 the news became more and more depressing. My father and Auntie Bet were now staying at JL's house in Streatham where he had constructed an elaborate shelter similar to the one in Basildon in which they spent every night. Each weekend visit brought news of yet another iconic building destroyed and the inevitable death or injury of friends. Whilst staying at JL's London house, they met some of his family. There was his son, Lew, who was unhappily married to Rose, who was away from London with their two children, Josephine and Phoebe. Then there were two sons-in-law, Eddie, who was married to JL's daughter, also Rose, and another Lew, who was married to Selena, always known as Lena. All three men worked in the garage. JL's son, Lew, didn't really have a function, he just wandered around and spent most afternoons asleep in the back of a cab; Eddie was the office manager and the other Lew drove a taxi.

My grandfather obtained permission to come to Basildon, but only on the understanding that he reported to the police station at Pitsea once a week. This was because he was still considered an enemy alien as he had never obtained British nationality. Once it was explained that he was blind, the police agreed to send an officer to visit him and one evening every week Detective Inspector Green would turn up, have a cup of tea and a chat, and go away again.

These visits came to an end in 1941 when Russia became our ally following the German invasion of the Soviet Union. A few days after that momentous event, it was announced that the Russian leader, Josef Stalin, would broadcast to the British people on Sunday evening. Of course, the speech would be in Russian, with a translation broadcast afterwards. But we had no need of interpreters, we had my grandfather. We all sat very quietly and listened, not daring to make a sound. At the end of the broadcast we turned to Grandpa and asked what had been said. After a few minutes' thought he said, 'You know what, those bloody communists have even changed the language!' By this time we had missed the translation so we never knew what Stalin said in that broadcast.

The German advance into Russia proceeded at an alarming rate and there was great distress in the house when we heard that Grandpa's home town of Minsk had been captured. Although he and his brothers had escaped at the turn of the century, they had left a large family behind and there was great concern for their fate. No trace was ever found of the Minsk family and it was assumed that they had ended their days in a gas chamber in Poland or been eliminated by the Russians earlier.

One positive outcome of the German advance to the east was that the threat of an imminent invasion of Britain had receded for the present.

Every day something new seemed to be happening at Joetta and I came home from school one day to find several armed police officers in the grounds. Apparently, they had learned of JL's pigeons and decided that homing pigeons were a security risk. They sealed the points of entry to the loft and shot every single bird as it returned in the evening. The adults were terribly distressed and I was confined to the house until everything had been cleared away. There was then the task of breaking the news to JL when he arrived on Saturday. He was extremely angry and took most of it out on Mr Bland. I never knew if JL's pigeons in London suffered the same fate.

Auntie Bet would save her washing for her weekend visits and during inclement weather a washing line would be rigged up in the kitchen. On this line would go several pairs of her black Directoire knickers. Somehow she always managed to peg them up in such a way that the access from the back door to the living room was obstructed. JL was a big man, tall and wide, and he never walked anywhere, he charged. He would come through the back door like a hurricane, only to have his progress blocked by a pair of wet knickers in his face. He would disengage himself and go on his way muttering unrepeatable curses – only to repeat the whole experience a few minutes later on his way out. Why she did it I never found out, but she did have a mind of her own.

But how did we entertain ourselves in those dark days? JL was a great raconteur and had a morbid interest in murder trials. If a high profile case was being tried at the Old Bailey he was always there for at least part of the trial. He also told stories of his time as a taxi driver before he had his own fleet. Particularly entertaining were the stories of the stage personalities he took home from the theatres. One particular actress who was a regular passenger was Violet Loraine, a musical theatre actress and singer who later went on to appear in films in the early thirties. The grown-ups were highly impressed that JL had mixed with such a famous personality.

It was at this time that I perfected the art of being neither seen nor heard. I would settle down in a corner of the room and listen, not uttering a sound. Eventually, somebody would realise I was still there and I would be sent to bed, but I learned a lot of grown-up things at a very young age and picked up a lot of gossip about friends and family, which meant very little then but made a lot of sense as I grew up.

The grown-ups used to speak in Yiddish if they wanted to discuss matters too delicate for my young ears, but it did not take me long to learn enough to get the gist of what they were saying. I never let on that I understood. Also their Yiddish wasn't all that fluent and every few words were in English. This helped me to understand what was being said.

Our main source of entertainment was the wireless and in true JL fashion we had a very elaborate radiogram. Our priority listening was the news, which was broadcast at least four times a day. I suppose it was some sort of security for the listeners that the newsreader always identified himself. The broadcast would open with, for example, 'This is the nine o'clock news, read by John Snagge'. Apart from the news, we would listen to programmes such as *Hi Gang* starring American comedy couple Ben Lyons and Bebe Daniels, accompanied by violinist and comedian Vic Oliver. Another comedy programme was *Happidrome* in the style of a Victorian music hall. There were three regular stars plus guests such as Max Miller, who was regularly being banned by the BBC because of his very suggestive material, and Sandy Powell, who I believe was partnered by a dog and had a catchphrase, 'Can you 'ear me mother?'. The show had a sign off song which went:

We three
Are working for the BBC
There's Enoch, Ramsbottom and me.

Of course one of the iconic comedy shows of the time was *ITMA* (short for *It's That Man Again*) which starred Tommy Handley accompanied by Jack Train, who played 'Colonel Chinstrap', a character who liked his drink. His catchphrase was always 'I don't mind if I do sir'. Another character was 'Mrs Mop', who played the office cleaner and her catchphrase was 'Can I do yer now sir?' The audience would wait expectantly for the catchphrase and then descend into howls of hysterical laughter. Catchphrases actually had their origin some years earlier, but they have been with us ever since and audience reactions are still the same.

A popular Saturday evening show was *In Town Tonight*, which opened with the sound of London traffic at Piccadilly Circus and the presenter would shout 'Stop!' followed by 'Once more we stop the roar of London's traffic to bring you people who are in town tonight.' I think the grown-ups found it interesting as they were familiar with the interviewees. At the end the announcer would shout 'Carry on London!' and the programme would end with the sound of traffic.

We also listened to such popular singers as Vera Lynn, singing the 'White Cliffs of Dover', and Gracie Fields, who was something of a national treasure with her 'Wish Me Luck As You Wave Me Goodbye' and 'Sally'. There was also Arthur Askey and Richard Murdoch in *Band Waggon* and various religious broadcasts. For more serious listeners there was *Saturday Night Theatre*, which always featured a play with a cast of well-known actors. On Monday nights we had

Henry Hall at 8 p.m. He always introduced his show with the same words, 'Good evening, this is Henry Hall and tonight is my guest night'. His signature tune was 'Here's to the Next Time...'

The Germans had managed to infiltrate our airwaves using a traitor named William Joyce broadcasting malicious propaganda from Berlin. He was known in this country as 'Lord Haw-Haw'. We only listened occasionally and I was cautioned never to tell anyone about it. Lord Haw-Haw was remarkably well-informed about what was going on in Britain and would give details of air raids and casualties within hours of their occurrence. I always found it difficult to understand how a man broadcasting from Germany could speak such perfect English. After the war, William Joyce was tried in London for treason and hanged. All in all, the radio provided some respite from the horrors of war and the depressing news at that time.

Apart from the radio my mother and Auntie Lill would spend hours talking to me about life before the war and they would get me to read parts of the day's newspaper. It was always the *Daily Mirror* and it wasn't long before I could master the front page, after which I moved on to the inside pages. Most news reports were supplemented by maps of the battle area, which helped me to learn geography. My favourite part of the paper was the strip cartoons page. There was Buck Ryan, a James Bond-type character, and his girlfriend, Zola; Belinda, who seemed to be a very talented little girl who succeeded at everything she attempted; the Ruggles family, who managed to cope with the crises of war remarkably well; and, of course, the infamous Jane who managed to lose her clothes every day – hardly suitable reading for a six-year-old! Lastly there was Useless Eustace who was a rather rotund, bowler-hatted individual who uttered a one-liner that the grown-ups found highly amusing.

In those days, what with the shortage of fuel and the need to conserve just about everything, the centre of family life was usually the dining table. We didn't have the use of armchairs so spent most of our leisure time sitting on upright chairs and talking, not only about the progress of the war, but about what was going on in the family and with family friends. These were my favourite times and having a very retentive memory, I have never forgotten much of what was talked about. Surprisingly, the need to sit on upright chairs meant that you rarely heard of anyone suffering from back problems. There may well be a lesson to be learned.

Uncle Harry finally got into the Army, having previously been in a reserved occupation, and was posted to a Royal Army Ordnance Corps (RAOC) base in Gloucester. For some reason he seemed to spend his weekend leave with us rather than his wife and children, although this may have been due to the distances involved. His family were in Melton Mowbray, which was a rather more difficult journey than Basildon. However, it might also have been the presence of a number of the aunts' girlfriends. One day, he turned up looking very dapper in regimental walking-out dress, which looked much smarter than the drab khaki that was common at that time. How he acquired this uniform was to become apparent all too soon.

The next we heard of him was a note from him headed Shepton Mallet Military Prison. Apparently he and the stores sergeant had been running a very lucrative scam involving blankets and it wasn't long before they found themselves before a court martial. I think he got about six weeks and that was the last he saw of his cushy job in the stores. Working in the stores was also how he managed to obtain his smart uniform.

Uncle Harry's misdemeanours didn't stop there. He had sadly inherited his father's proclivity for womanising and somehow managed to get involved with a very young local girl in Gloucester, who was well below the age of consent. The girl became pregnant and her irate parents wanted the commanding officer to have Uncle Harry prosecuted. The Army obviously didn't want a scandal and immediately shipped my wayward uncle off to the Middle East, where he spent the rest of the war. What sins he committed out there were known only to him.

JL owned many properties in Basildon and technically next door, although almost a quarter of a mile away, was Lewis Villa (named after his son), occupied by another Jewish family, named Wolf. They were Londoners and Mr Wolf used to commute to London each day. They had a son about my age who I befriended and my mother used to visit them regularly. Inevitably, the country life became too much for Mrs Wolf and the family decided to return to London. This was wonderful news for my mother and within days we were packed and ready to move in. This was to be home to Mum, Dad and me for the next nine years. Grandma's furniture came out of store together with the few items rescued from Hayter Road and this meant that my father could be with us all the time and commute to London every day. To have her own home was heaven to my mother and from a two-room flat in London's East End, she now had a six-room house in its own grounds. We had mains gas, water and electricity with an indoor toilet. Drainage was still by cesspit and we shared this facility with our next-door neighbours, Basildon Stores. The problem was that sometimes blockages occurred and my father had to shift the blockage, which involved a lot of bad language and the most appalling smells. Fortunately this did not happen too often. The other downside was the smell from the pit in the summer. This did evoke complaints from the neighbours.

5

LEWIS VILLA

Lewis Villa was a wooden shiplap house with a glass veranda on two sides built in the 'plotlands' style common in the area. The internal walls and ceilings were all constructed of asbestos sheeting, which made fixing anything to the walls virtually impossible. There was also a balcony leading off one of the upstairs bedrooms, which became my room after the war. The house was set to the back of the plot, which was probably about an acre in size. At the front was a huge lawn, the size of a tennis court, to one side of the path. On the other side was a vegetable garden in which we grew most of our vegetables. Beyond the lawn was a large orchard, comprising over thirty pear trees together with a few apple and plum trees. There was also a grape vine, but the grapes were not really suitable for eating. We used to sell the pears during the late summer and I seemed to spend all my spare time either up a ladder picking fruit or delivering it. One result of this was that I acquired a dislike of pears which has persisted to this day. Because the house was a lot older than Joetta, it lacked some of the more luxurious amenities, such as a fridge or an immersion heater, to which we had become accustomed. Water in the kitchen could only be heated by a back boiler behind the lounge fire, which we hardly ever used. Hot water for the kitchen sink was

A photograph of Lewis Villa from around 1941-42, slightly damaged because of its age.

boiled in a kettle. The bath had a gas water heater which was very efficient. In the kitchen we had a gas cooker and a rather antiquated kitchen range, which was black and had to be polished with Zebo every day. It was not very efficient and provided very little heat, but we could keep a kettle on the top so that we always had hot water. The oven was quite useless and was never used. I don't think Lewis Villa was built by JL as it was a rather picturesque house, whereas JL tended to build quite ugly, uninspiring properties. I suspect that he bought it with all its land and developed the site by building the shop on one part and Selena, a bungalow named after his daughter and based on a Canadian log cabin design, on another part. That would account for a very odd-shaped plot on which our house was placed. One day whilst we were digging in one of the flower beds at the front of the house we hit solid concrete. When we asked JL what it was for, he told Dad that he had planned to have a filling station adjacent to the shop and underneath our lawn was a giant storage tank intended for petrol. Naturally, I was curious and with my friend, John Willie, managed to lift a manhole cover in front of the house. As we were looking down into the tank out came my mother in a panic as she thought I was about to fall in. We also discovered that our house had once contained a cellar which had been filled in. I spent a lot of time trying to find any sign of the cellar, without success.

One advantage of having our own house was being able to have visitors to stay. Auntie Jane had gone to work at a residential children's home in Middlesex and was a regular visitor. I always enjoyed her visits because she would take me out and do things that my mother wasn't interested in. Also, Kitty would visit with Doris and Alan once or twice a year. I looked forward to their visits as Kitty was always good fun, much to the dismay of my father who was rather possessive of my mother and didn't like her mixing with anyone. I think he also resented the extra work imposed on my mother and, being rather mean, counted the cost of having visitors. This was sad really because Dad had a great sense of humour and he got up to some wicked practical jokes, some of which I managed to participate in.

Our move also meant that there was more room at Joetta for guests and during the summer of 1941 every weekend saw different people, mainly female, visiting. They could escape the stress of London and enjoy swimming, horse riding and country walks, all for free. Two regular visitors were the Benson sisters, Esther and Millie, who were very old family friends. On one particular Sunday morning Esther was riding a rather large horse. It was a lovely animal which had been trained as a police horse and should have been very docile. However on this occasion he had had enough of his rider and decided to throw her off. This was not unusual, but the horse chose his spot well. At the top of the field where this took place was a large pile of chicken manure which Mr Bland used to add to when he cleaned out the poultry houses. The sun had hardened the surface and it looked deceptively solid. Sadly, this was not the case and just below the surface was noxious liquid manure. Esther landed right in the middle of this and went straight through the outer crust to land with something of a splash. Although she appealed for help, nobody responded. Amid a great deal of laughter from the onlookers, which I'm sure included the horse, Esther managed to pick herself up and get back onto solid ground. She was not a pretty sight and she smelt awful. I think she was taken to the stable where she stripped off and Millie brought clean clothes to her. No more riding for her that weekend. In fact, I don't think she ever got on a horse again.

JL's son Lew was a frequent visitor and he would turn up at odd times, saying he wanted to look at the horses. How he managed to look at horses in the dark was a bit of a mystery, but perhaps it was the aunts who were the attraction. Lew was an instant target for Dad's practical jokes and one Sunday morning we were in what we thought was Lew's bedroom in Joetta and Dad showed me how to make an 'apple pie' bed. Not content with that, he hid one of Lew's shoes in the bed. Lew was due to travel to London on the Monday morning on the workmen's bus, but when the bus stopped outside Joetta, Lew came rushing out in his slippers saying he had lost one of his shoes. The bus wouldn't wait so Lew was in trouble with his father when he finally got to the garage. It didn't take much intelligence to work out that if Lew had slept in his own bed he would have found his shoe. So where did he sleep that night? Did Dad have an ulterior motive for his actions? Lew never knew who had played that joke on him. Lew was a frequent visitor to our house and I always enjoyed his visits. He would tell us stories about his father, many of which were hilarious.

My mother had to help out with Grandpa at Joetta, so she still spent a lot of time there and I used to stop in on my way home from school. She also used to spend whole days there when Auntie Lill went to London.

By mid-1941 the realities of war caught up with Basildon and the swimming pool was requisitioned by the fire service as an emergency water supply in case of an incendiary attack. Most of the usable land was taken over and ploughed up for the cultivation of wheat. JL got rid of most of the horses and things became a lot quieter. The biggest loss to JL was the reduction in the petrol allowance. This meant that he could no longer drive to Basildon and had to resort to the train. This was a major operation for him because he did not travel light. There were always at least two suitcases and two very large cardboard boxes, each of which contained several dozen eggs, on his return journey to London. One weekend he decided that he would make the journey by road. The eastern limit for travel by London taxis was Romford and he had one of his own vehicles take him there. Earlier the same day, Mr Bland set out by horse and cart to meet him at Romford. It must have been a marathon task; the horse they used was quite old and certainly not used to a forty-mile round trip. I think it took most of the day and was never repeated. However, on one Sunday, he decided that instead of ordering a local taxi, he would travel to Pitsea Station by horse and cart with Auntie Bet in charge of driving back once he was on the train. Mum and I decided to go along to keep her company. For some reason on the return journey, Auntie Bet's attention must have wandered as we passed the Broadway cinema in Pitsea and the horse mounted the pavement and made a beeline for the queue waiting for the doors to open. Auntie Bet dropped the reins with no idea what to do, my mother just screamed, the people in the cinema queue started to panic and I had the task of jumping down, calming the horse and getting us back on the road. Fortunately the horse was a really docile animal and in a few minutes we were on our way again. That was something else that was never repeated.

6

FRIENDS AND NEIGHBOURS

In 1941 I was getting on for seven years old and starting to make friends with the local children. Our part of Church Road was quite well populated; next door was the shop and next to that was another of JL's properties, Selena. Beyond that was a farm owned by Will Buckley, who ran it with his brother, Harry, who was also his neighbour. Will had a daughter, Jean, who was two years older than me. Harry had two sons, Bob, who was in his teens, and John, who was the same age as Jean. Opposite Lewis Villa was a smallholding run by Mr and Mrs Brodie and they had a son, John Willie, about two years my senior. The Brodies were a reclusive family and considered very pro-German by the residents. They mixed with nobody, although I became friends with John, who was a very clever boy and taught me all about electricity and wireless at a very young age. I think it was a country thing that families who did not mix were considered odd and subject to, in many cases, malicious speculation. How the pro-German suspicion came about I have no idea, but it stuck until well after the war. I do not ever remember Mr Brodie leaving his farm and his wife only ever seemed to visit the shop opposite. On the rare occasion when she caught the bus, Mr Brodie did not allow her to wait with others at the bus stop; he would stop the bus right outside their house and when it stopped he would summon her from the shadows of the house to board the bus. Actually, Mrs Brodie was a very nice lady but she dressed as if still in the Victorian age, with black woollen stockings, black skirts almost down to her ankles, black lace up shoes and her hair in plaits coiled round her ears. From what Willie said, his father was a sadistic bully and he made it clear that it was just a matter of time before he was old enough to retaliate.

Further down the road opposite Joetta was a row of small, semi-detached houses called Alford Villas. These were owned equally by Will and Harry Buckley and rented out. No. 1 Alford Villas was occupied by the Humphreys family. Mr Humphreys had a wooden leg as a result of injuries sustained in the First World War and was something of a bully to his wife and children, Lucy and Alfie. They were both older than me but rather simple. I suppose today we would call them slow learners. Alfie was in our gang; a tall, gangly sort of boy who had a heart of gold. However, he was never far from trouble. A few of us used to explore the deserted old manor house at the top of the road and we decided to remove some of the internal doors to make a raft to sail on the lake in the grounds. We made a good job of it and had a lot of fun on the lake, but one day turned up to find a rival gang had untied the raft and it was languishing in the middle of the lake. We pondered over how to recover it when Alfie insisted that with a good run he could jump onto the raft from the bank. He walked back as far as he could and started running. At the edge of the lake he took off and as predicted landed right in the middle of the raft. Unfortunately, his momentum kept him going and he went straight off the other side and into the lake. It wasn't very deep but he was soaked to the skin. He waded back to the side but we sent him back to recover the raft; after all, he couldn't get any wetter. Now Alfie was terrified of his parents, particularly his father, so we were faced with the problem of how to get him dry. Our solution was to get him to run round and round the lake in the hope that the motion would dry his clothes. It didn't work and his clothes seemed to be shrinking before our eyes. We tried to think of ways to smuggle him into the house without being spotted by his father, but there was only one way in which led directly into the kitchen where his father would be sitting; front doors were never used in the country. A rather bedraggled Alfie had no choice but to face the wrath of his father. He later told us that he had beaten him mercilessly with his walking stick and sent him to bed without his supper. Alfie eventually ran away and joined a visiting fair. Surprisingly, these things did happen. We saw him once or twice when the fair came but he never saw his parents again.

At No. 2 lived the Hammond family. They were very pleasant and had a daughter, Evelyn, who was about a year younger than me, and a much younger child, Raymond. Their neighbours at No. 3 were Doris and Albert Wenham who had twin boys five years my senior, Mick and David. They were our gang leaders and over the years David and I became good friends. The Wenhams were from the East End and my mother and Doris became friends, a friendship which lasted the rest of their lives. Doris was an outworker for a firm of dressmakers in Southend and Mum would help out when she was busy. The Lewis family lived next door at No. 4 but they didn't mix at all. They had a son, Terry, who was younger than me but I don't recall much about him. An old couple lived at No. 5 and I don't think I ever knew their names. At No. 6 was the Robbins family whose son, Ken, was two years my senior. He had two younger sisters but I cannot remember their names. Ken was in our gang when his mother would let him out. Next door at No. 7 was Mrs Fearne, who had a baby daughter. Her husband was in the Army and being much younger than all the other women did not mix with them. Finally, at No. 8, was the Rowe family. Mrs Rowe had four sons, possibly conceived with three separate fathers. Ronnie was the eldest and he eventually joined the Merchant Navy, becoming first mate on a barge which travelled along the coast. There was a story put about by his mother that Ronnie's barge was used in the filming of *Great Expectations* and he had dated Jean Simmons, who starred in the film. He was a handsome boy so it might have happened. Certainly there was a barge in one of the scenes and Jean Simmons was about his age. Next to him was Cecil, a year older than me. He was one of my close friends and in our gang. He had two younger brothers, Dickie and Johnny, but no father was ever in evidence.

Alford Villas were tiny houses, two up, two down, with no internal sanitation. The second bedroom was tiny and it is a mystery how a whole family was accommodated. In many cases the downstairs front room was used as a bedroom occupied by the parents with the children sleeping upstairs.

My other friend was another Buckley; this one was Clive. His father, Alf, was the brother of Will and Harry but he had very little to do with them. They lived on the edge of Will's farm and their bungalow was reached along Springfield Road, which was nothing more than a mud path. His mother, May, used to do smocking which was a very skilled occupation, used mainly on children's dresses. Clive was not part of our gang, which meant I had divided loyalties and had to juggle two friendship groups. Clive and I became very close friends, being almost the same age. We attended the same schools and later we both joined the RAF for our National Service. Sadly Clive died, aged nineteen, in a motorcycle accident on his way back to camp from a weekend we had spent together.

There were, of course, other friends at school and due to the very wide catchment area, these came from further afield. There was John Davey, who lived with his parents and older brother about half a mile away, but visiting him was not without hazard. Their bungalow was alongside the railway line and the story went that Mr Davey used to carry his building materials from London on the train and throw them out as he passed his building site. I never found out if that was true, but I do know that he always left the train at Laindon and walked along the track collecting whatever was lying around on his way. Their bungalow was a real 'house that Jack built'. But it was the access that was dangerous. It was surrounded by a stream, across which were two railway sleepers. It was necessary to cross this 'bridge' without falling in the stream. How they made the journey in the dark I have no idea as the drop was about 8-10ft. Mr Davey always seemed to have whatever was needed and when John told him we wanted a flagpole, one appeared the following day looking remarkably like a telegraph pole.

Living quite close to the Davey family were the Hales family, comprising John and Hannah together with daughters Barbara and Joan, the latter being my age. Mum had been at school with Hannah, who was older than her, and also her sister, who lived quite close. They used to get together at least once a week to reminisce over their school days but inevitably my mother managed to fall out with Hannah's sister. John was quite an entrepreneur and worked as a postman in London, although I don't think he did much in the way of delivering letters. He grew large quantities of flowers and vegetables which he took to work and sold. He also took large amounts of our fruit and eggs so Dad and I would be at his house most Sundays making deliveries and buying some of his produce. They were a lovely family, although John did slip from grace by having a liaison with one of his female colleagues. The affair would have continued undetected had fate not intervened. Sadly the lady was killed in a bombing raid and when her locker was opened a bundle of letters from John were found. I think the whole thing was covered up but John's lack of actual work for the Post Office was noticed and he had to buckle down to delivering mail. His family never found out and I think Dad was the only person in whom he confided.

Our local primary school was situated about three miles away in Vange but could really only be reached directly by school bus. The journey involved walking about half a mile to the end of Church Road and catching the bus which visited outlying villages before depositing us at school. If we missed the bus we had to walk across the fields which was OK in the summer, but in the cold and wet weather we made sure we didn't miss the bus.

We all attended Vange School and I have already mentioned John Scorer, who was a truly dedicated teacher, as were most of the staff. All the male teachers had been called up but he had a good team and I progressed well through the school. The target was the eleven-plus, or the scholarship as we knew it. I never understood the term eleven-plus; I was ten when I took it so preferred the word scholarship. Passing that led to a grammar school education and Mr Scorer would pick six or eight children who he saw as likely to succeed and coach them himself in the run up to the exam. Clive and I were part of that group in our year and of the six selected, four of us were successful. However that was some years in the future and there was most of the war to get through. There were brick-built shelters at school and I only remember going into them once during an air raid. There were other incidents which involved girls in our class, but that had nothing to do with air raids, simply curiosity by both boys and girls.

Being the only Jewish child in the school had its problems; my parents never insisted that I should not take part in religious activities, but prejudice that I did not understand had to be contended with. Although this came from the children it must have originated in the home from the parents. It usually took the form of taunts, such as we were only fighting the war because of the Jews, which I learnt to ignore. The worse times were in the run up to Easter when we were recalling the story of the Crucifixion in school. Apparently I was personally responsible for what happened nearly 2,000 years ago and would be beaten up on a regular basis. Even my 'friends' would join in, which I found rather confusing. I never said anything at home but one day I returned from school in a bit of a mess and my mother got the whole story out of me. She said nothing but the following day after lunch the whole school was assembled in the hall and Mr Scorer castigated everybody present, threatening dire consequences if there was a repeat of this bullying. My worry apart from being singled out as a victim was that there would be repercussions but the opposite happened; boys who were more senior and who I hardly knew came up to me and promised to deal with anybody who bothered me in the future. I was something of a hero for a few days. My mother told me when I got home that she went to the school in the morning and told Mr Scorer what had happened. He was horrified. Not only was he not prepared to put up with such conduct in his school but one of his closest friends was a Jewish Member of Parliament and he felt he had let him down. The Scorers had a daughter, Eunice, who was at university at that time and she used to help out at school during her vacations. Eunice became a doctor and specialised in eye surgery. Years later JL was in hospital having his cataracts treated and Eunice was his surgeon. When he found out who her father was he started to tell her the story but she interrupted him, saying she knew all about it and it was an event her father had never forgotten.

The war progressed and we learned to live with disturbed nights spent in the cupboard under the stairs, food shortages and clothes rationing. My father commuted to London six days a week, leaving at 6.30 a.m. and returning around 7.30 p.m. The local bus service was Campbells Coaches, run by three brothers who did most of the driving. Dick Campbell used to drive the workmen's bus which went past our house to the top of the road, then turned round to start the journey to Pitsea Station. If Dick passed our house and saw no signs of life he would stop the bus and knock on the door to wake Dad up. He would then wait outside the house on the return leg until Dad was on board. Dick also drove the school bus. He was a popular driver with all the passengers but he had one very unpleasant tendency; he had an aversion to personal hygiene. He wore the same clothes every day, apparently never took a bath and his feet had a smell which had to be experienced to be believed. It was said that you didn't just hear his bus approaching, you could smell Dick before you heard the sound of the engine. Almost all the men commuted to London and every day wives would say goodbye to their loved ones, never knowing if they would return that night. Looking back it is hard to understand how they coped, but cope they did.

7

MY DOMESTIC DUTIES

Once we were settled in at Lewis Villa, JL decided we should become poultry farmers. He installed a chicken house in our orchard, erected fences and we acquired about forty hens. My father and I took to this new venture with enthusiasm but my mother was not so keen. However the constant supply of eggs made it all rather more acceptable, not only because we had fresh eggs on the table but the surplus was like currency. Eggs were in very short supply and whilst they could be sold at the exorbitant price of 4s a dozen, they could also be exchanged for other food not readily available. As a result we never went short of anything and lived quite well in spite of the severity of rationing and the total absence of imported fruit such as bananas and oranges. Come Christmas and Easter, one of the chickens would be killed and eaten. Dad could not do this himself and I had to take the selected chicken to one of our neighbours, who would wring its neck. I then had to rush back home whilst it was still warm to do the plucking, which was much more difficult if the bird was cold. I used to hate the plucking, but somehow it became my job. Once the bird was plucked it would be hung in the larder for a week to ten days until it was 'high' and then it was prepared and cooked. I wonder what the food hygiene people of today would have said had they been around then. We always purchased about two dozen fertilized eggs in early spring and usually got around twelve chicks which went on to grow into laying birds and replace those that had passed their laying time and were killed. The feeding of the chickens was my job and they were initially fed on a 'mash' mixture, but later we were introduced to Tottenham pudding. This was made from the food waste put out in swill bins on London streets and processed into slabs of feed. The name came from the North London suburb where it was processed. It looked horrible, smelt horrible and was like toffee to handle. It was cut up into chunks and fed to the chickens, who seemed to enjoy it. Egg production improved, although the eggs had a slight tang to them, as did the meat. The important thing was to avoid touching it as the stains were very difficult to get rid of.

In those days, and this had nothing to do with war, fruit was very seasonal and the only way to enjoy fruits such as plums out of season was to preserve them. The method was to boil the fruit slowly in a preserving pan, which resembled a giant saucepan, and whilst hot place it in 'Kilner' jars, which were like oversized jam jars with a glass lid and a rubber washer. The glass top was sealed by a metal spring clip. Later versions replaced the spring clip with a screw cap. Properly done, fruit preserved this way would last for years.

Much of our fruit was not really suitable to eat until around Christmastime and in order to preserve the hard fruit such as pears and apples, we utilised an old chest; the drawers were lined with layers of newspaper on which the fruit was laid very carefully, then covered with more layers of newspaper. Periodically, the fruit was turned and checked. If any had become bruised in the picking they were removed. By Christmas we had a good selection of winter apples and pears, some of which we sold. These were 'country ways' and had probably been practised for generations.

My mother still retained the 'townie' attitude and did not like coming into contact with anything agricultural. Being something of a torment, I would catch one of the chickens, quietly open the back door and push it in. It wasn't long before I heard the screams and the threat of dire retribution when she caught me. The punishment usually took the form of being hit with a wet dishcloth but to me it was worth it. Even Dad used to laugh when she told him what I had done. I think he was becoming aware that I had inherited his sense of humour. It was this experience of chicken farming which later gave me the idea to go to agricultural college and become a farmer. I nursed this ambition for many years but there was no way my mother would ever let that particular aspiration become a reality.

Although we had all of my grandmother's furniture, we did not have a radio and it was impossible to buy one. Uncle Harry's family had relocated to Melton Mowbray so, after an exchange of correspondence with him in Egypt, we were able to borrow the radio from their house in Dagenham. For some reason we kept it in the lounge and we had to listen to it from the kitchen. I never understood the reason for this. I suppose a radio was some sort of status symbol and had to be displayed in the 'best room'. Why my parents didn't contact Kitty, who was living in Melton Mowbray, I never knew. But that's families.

Not having the benefit of today's labour saving devices, I had to do my share of household tasks, particularly during school holidays. Monday was the worst day for me as it was washing day. A lot of houses had a 'copper', which was like a giant cauldron built, not of copper, but brick and cement. At the bottom was a fire box which, when lit, would heat the water in which the dirty laundry was soaking. This would go on until the washing was clean. Stories abounded about suet puddings being cooked in the copper with the washing but I never knew the truth of those stories.

We had no such amenity; we filled a small tin bath with boiling water, put the dirty garments in the bath and then, with the aid of a washboard and hard soap, each item would be scrubbed until clean. After the tin bath came my job, which was the mangling. Most households had a mangle and the majority had two rubber rollers through which the wet washing was fed by the use of a handle. I was the one turning the handle. Not only was it hard work but our mangle was so old that half the rubber had broken away from the rollers so that only about half the water was ever wrung out. This meant several attempts until Mum thought all the water had been removed.

Not only was this hard work but it always seemed to happen at lunchtime. My mother would not make lunch until the mangling was finished and I used to make a great drama about dying from starvation. Sometimes I would pretend to faint over the mangle but it was a waste of time. No lunch until the mangling was finished.

Another of my allocated and much hated domestic chores was Sunday morning baking. My job was mixing the flour and fat together for whatever Mum was making; biscuits, cake or pastry. This was a really messy job that seemed to take forever and encroached severely on the time I wanted to spend in the garden with Dad. To this day, I do not really like cooking.

8

WHAT ARE WE QUEUING FOR?

Naturally my mother still yearned for the excitement of London and whilst this was not possible on a regular basis, we settled into a Saturday routine. This would follow a three-week cycle. The first trip would be to Southend, followed by Romford the following week and Noak Hill to visit Grandma on the third Saturday. Then the routine would be repeated.

When we did visit London during the school holidays we would usually head for Oxford Street and perhaps meet up with Auntie Jane. After the shops we would visit Lyon's Corner House for lunch, followed by a visit to the cinema. Despite the shortages there was a limited amount of stock in the shops, although sometimes buying the more sought after items was not easy. We had that great phenomenon of the war – the queue. The British were, and in fact still are, very disciplined about queuing and there was a simple routine; if you saw a queue, you joined it. What was actually on sale didn't matter; if there was a queue it must be worth the wait. On one occasion we were in Oxford Street and were to meet Auntie Jane when my mother saw a line of people. True to form she joined the line and you then asked the person in front what they were queuing for. Nobody knew so I was sent to find the head of the queue and what people were buying. Eventually I found the start of the line which was outside a shop called Jax, a chain of small shops selling lingerie. On this day the shop had a supply of silk stockings, hence the queue. I could understand the logic of the queue but never understood how word got round in the first place. I think we spent half the morning just to get one pair of stockings and I was really fed up. Somehow I managed to find Auntie Jane and she took me off somewhere, probably Hyde Park. Silk stockings were in short supply because silk was used in the manufacture of parachutes. From time to time somebody would acquire an old parachute and the panels would be shared out. Many young ladies walked up the aisle in a pure silk wedding dress and this material was also used for silk underwear or nightdresses. An added bonus was not having to use valuable coupons. The only parachute silk that came our way was not white but camouflage and I can't imagine any lady would be prepared to wear green and brown underwear. We had some strange looking cushion covers for many years.

On another occasion we joined a queue outside Lawleys at Oxford Circus. Lawleys sold china so it was just a matter of waiting until we reached the head of the queue to find out what we were queuing for. On this occasion it was 'Green Dawn' plates, which we still have to this day. Sometimes we would pass a queue outside Hamleys, the world famous toy shop in Regent Street, but I was never allowed to even pause, let alone join that line.

Every visit to London revealed more bomb damage and this was rather depressing for my mother. Well known landmarks were gone forever and in so many instances all that were left standing where houses had been bombed were the chimney stacks and these looked grotesque just standing isolated on a bomb site. Sometimes a section of wall would be left standing with perhaps a door in the middle of that wall on the first or second floor. There would even be wallpaper still hanging from what was left of the walls. Most of these were quite quickly demolished as they were considered dangerous.

As we usually arrived in London very early and before the shops were open, we would visit Kitty's mother, Mrs Silver, who lived in

Whitechapel in the infamous 'buildings'. These were the so-called slums that were demolished after the war to make room for tower blocks. Mrs Silver lived in a semi-basement flat comprising a living room and bedroom with a small scullery curtained off from the main room. There was no sanitation and she shared a toilet on the ground floor landing with her neighbours. Similarly there was one sink with a cold water tap shared by the same residents. She was a very pleasant lady and always made us welcome. Sadly she felt the same about Harry as my family thought about Kitty and did not have a good word to say about him. How my mother held her tongue I have no idea; reticence wasn't in her makeup. Mrs Silver used to work for a local factory specialising in handmade cigarettes. She was an outworker and spent all the hours there were stuffing tobacco into these cigarettes and earning a pittance. She always said that most of what she earned went in buying clothes for Doris and Alan.

We would go to Southend by train from Pitsea and there was always the same ritual; out of the station, turn left up the High Street to Victoria Circus and left onto London Road to look in Percy Raven's window. This was a high class store which is still in business to this day. We would then cross the road and walk down to Lyons tea shop for a roll and butter with a cup of tea. Sometimes we would pop into Keddies department store but for some reason browsing inside stores was not something my mother did very often, she preferred window shopping. Then on down the High Street towards the pier. Here the road was closed off by a barbed wire barrier, so we would cross over and head back to the station in time to meet Dad from London, sometimes looking at Brightwell's window on the way. We would then go to one of three cinemas to see the film my mother had chosen. It was always her choice. After the film we would catch the train home. I hated those visits to Southend, mainly because we had to look in every shop window irrespective of what they sold and, of course, the display did not change which meant we would be looking at the same window display for months, sometimes years. I knew every shop in Southend High Street and was able to recite the contents of every window.

We bought very little because by now almost everything was rationed, including clothes. We each had an allocation of clothing coupons and once they were used up it was necessary to wait for the next allocation. However, there were concessions for children's clothes. This was the age of 'make do and mend' and my mother was a genius at making clothes out of old or worn-out garments. At one time she got very ambitious and decided to make a jacket for me out of one of her old skirts. The finished article was superb and I remember the teacher standing me up in front of the class to admire her handiwork. Garments had to be patched and darned and quite often it was difficult to tell if any original part of a sock existed. My mother was expert at making new collars for Dad's shirts. She would cut a piece off the tail and used that. This worked well if the shirt had no stripes; otherwise the stripes usually went the wrong way. The shortened shirt tail was lengthened by any piece of fabric that was handy. I was saved from many of the more extreme repairs because I was growing quite fast and was always in need of new clothes. In those days boys wore boots which were usually fitted with metal heels and toecaps to prevent wear on the leather. They were uncomfortable and noisy and I used to look forward to Saturdays when I could wear shoes. Sadly for my parents, my feet wouldn't stop growing which meant I always seemed to be hobbling about in shoes and boots that were far too small.

The family really embraced 'make do and mend'; worn-out knitted jumpers were picked apart and the wool used to knit a new garment; if there was not sufficient wool, another colour would be added, resulting in some rather bizarre colour combinations. My mother was not a great knitter but she decided to knit socks for me. She was so slow that I had always outgrown the socks long before their completion. But I still had to wear them, no matter how tight. Auntie Bet embarked on a rug making project which involved cutting old worn-out clothes into strips and, using a tool similar to a crochet hook, these strips were woven onto a canvas mesh. She used mainly old items of underwear and stockings, which resulted in a black and brown colour combination without any real design. I think the war ended long before the rug was ever finished.

With sweets in such short supply, my father decided to make some marzipan sweets using soya flour as the main ingredient. As sweets were on the menu I was an enthusiastic helper. I am not sure what the finished articles were supposed to be but we ate the sweets as fast as Dad made them and I don't think the rest of the family even got a taste. I have no idea what the ingredients were, but I spent most of the night being sick and was too ill to go to school the next day. We never made sweets again and after all those years, I still cannot eat marzipan sweets.

On one of the three Saturdays we would visit Romford, where the routine was the same as Southend. I suppose the main difference was how we got there. We would catch the London train to Upminster and then change onto the 'push-pull' line, which was a single track terminating at Romford. As the name suggests, the engine pushed the carriages one way and pulled them on the return journey.

As with Southend, we would come out of the station, turn left and examine every shop down as far as the market. My mother wasn't one for markets but there was a huge covered area which we had to go round before heading back on the other side of the High Street, stopping at Lyon's for tea and a roll before meeting my father off the London train. Then came the ritual visit to the cinema before catching the train home. I never discovered if Dad ever got any lunch.

The third Saturday was my favourite when we went to visit Grandma at Noak Hill. The journey was almost the same as going to Romford except that we got off the 'push-pull' train one stop earlier at Emerson Park where we caught a bus to Noak Hill.

My father was Grandma's favourite son and although she had borne six children, I was her only grandson, which clearly made me very special to her. Grandma was a wonderful cook and there was certainly no shortage of food at Manor Farm. Uncle Jim was a great character and would take me out to his shed, where he would show me his shotguns and whatever game he had shot and was hanging until ripe. On one particular day I caused great consternation when I picked up one of the guns and pointed it at my mother as she came to call us for lunch. I never knew what happened next but suddenly Uncle Jim had knocked me to the floor and grabbed the gun. It was the only time I remember him being angry with me. When he had calmed down he explained very forcibly that you never point a gun at anything unless you intend to pull the trigger. I argued that the gun wasn't loaded but he asked me how I knew that. Of course, I had just assumed that to be the case. I never knew how my mother felt looking down the barrel of that gun. Uncle Jim soon calmed down and we had to go through two rituals before lunch. First I wanted to see his pocket watch, which to me was unusual because the actual watch was contained in a silver case and to wind it there was a very small key, very much like a miniature clock key. That watch is now one of my treasured possessions. After the watch, I had to feel in his other waistcoat pocket where there was always a sixpenny piece.

Once lunch was over it was time to go across the road to the farm and what we did there very much depended on the season. Sometimes we would trek up to the spinney and I would pick bluebells, which usually wilted before we got home. In the late summer it was harvest time and I would be in the thick of things, helping with the stacking of the stooks or, if threshing was in progress, helping to fork the stooks up into the machine. There were no combine harvesters in those days. The wheat was cut by machine and stacked to dry until the threshing contractor arrived. He would tour the farms with a traction engine which operated the threshing machine by a series of drive belts. This was all very high-tech for the 1940s. Some of the smaller farms still used a scythe to cut the wheat and threshing was by beating the grain and allowing the wind to blow away the husks, leaving the corn. The standing crops were a haven for rats, mice and rabbits. Normally the cutting was carried out in a decreasing circle until the machine reached the middle of the field. As the circle got smaller, the creatures would eventually make a run for it. The farm workers were ready for them and used their caps to catch whatever they could. I found it fascinating as they could end up catching anything. There was very little thought for personal hygiene, as the cap went straight back on the head even if they had just caught a rat with it. You could always tell the experienced 'old hands' because they tied string round their trousers to stop creatures climbing up their legs.

Grandma was a great stickler for manners and protocol and before I went over to the farm, she would lecture me on how I should conduct myself. I was always dressed in my best suit and wore my cap. My instructions were that when I met Jamie, who was Uncle Jim's grandson, I had to raise my cap and say, 'Good afternoon, Master James'. Uncle Jim said nothing when I assured her on my return that I had obeyed her instructions. I didn't know how to explain to her that with Jamie in the cow shed stripped to the waist with his arm up some intimate part of a cow's anatomy, it was hardly the time and place to observe the social niceties.

Uncle Percy's wife was Elaine and I always went to see her in the main house. She was a lovely, gentle lady and would spend time talking to me about school and the progress I was making. Then she would take me upstairs to one of the attic rooms which was crammed with books which had been Jamie's. I was allowed to select one book to take with me and she always made sure that my choice was right for my age. Elaine's sister married Prince Birabongse, who was a very successful pre-war motor racing driver. He was apparently a grandson of the King of Siam, whose story was vividly portrayed in *The King and I*.

By the time we got back to Grandma's I was not the smartly turned out little boy of two or three hours previously. This was particularly so if Uncle Jim asked me to pick some cucumbers. The problem with this simple task was that the cucumber plants were grown on top of a giant manure heap which I had to climb. This caused me to pong a bit, apart from being grubby. My mother used to tell me off before giving me a quick clean up, but we used to get some funny looks on the way home.

The last job of the day was to get the cows that were grazing on our side of the road into the milking parlour. This involved opening gates on both sides of the road and getting a couple of cows to lead the way. Once started, the rest of the herd would follow and all we had to do was chase up a few stragglers. The road hardly had any traffic and once over the road they would find their own way to the parlour. On one occasion, when Uncle Jim was ill and confined to his bed, he told me to get the cows over the road on my own. Looking back this was a rather dangerous exercise. I was smaller than the cows and all I had was a stick to push them along. However, I managed it without mishap, although we never told the grown-ups what I had done.

My dad would arrive during the afternoon and Grandma always had a bowl of hot water and Pears soap ready for him to wash as soon as he walked through the door. One task Uncle Jim regularly asked him to perform was to cut his nails. There was nothing special about that except it wasn't scissors that were used, it was a sheep shearing tool. That was sight I had never seen before or since.

I once asked Uncle Jim if he had ever travelled and in his broad Essex accent he replied 'I went to "farrin parts" once but I couldn't understand what they said so I came home'. It turned out that he had once gone to Chelmsford, which was about twenty miles away. He never travelled any further than that in all his eighty-plus years.

Sadly Grandma died in 1944 and we lost touch with the Quilters, mainly because my father was not a family-orientated person.

9

FIRE WATCHING

However, back to the early years of the war. One day there was a knock at our front door and standing there with his back to us was an Army officer. When he turned round it was JL wearing the uniform of a Home Guard captain, complete with a rather serious-looking revolver in its holster. We never knew why he joined but it only lasted about a week. I think as soon as he learned it was a bit more than dressing up he resigned.

The Home Guard (immortalised in *Dad's Army*) was mainly comprised of those men too old to join the armed forces or young men awaiting call-up. They were trained to defend essential services and assist the Army when required. They were not at all the comical individuals seen on television. One day my father received a letter calling him up for service with the Home Guard. For some reason he didn't want to join as he seemed to have an aversion to uniforms. He would not even let me join the Boy Scouts. He decided to appeal and went before a tribunal and argued that his time was better spent doing what the government were always urging us to do – dig for victory. He won his appeal but they did suggest that he should contribute something to the war effort, so he became a fire watcher in London. This involved staying overnight once every week or ten days and, from a high vantage point, spotting where the incendiary bombs were falling and directing the fire services. This was not very onerous and seemed to be more of a social event until one night in March 1943 when a terrible disaster occurred at Bethnal Green underground station. From the start of the Blitz it had been the habit of many families to take refuge in the underground stations; because of their depth they were considered the safest places to be. The platforms had been equipped with rows of two or three-tiered bunks and the evenings became very much party evenings. There would be singing and dancing and presumably a supply of alcohol found its way into the shelter. It was one way to be safe and put the terror of what was going on above out of mind for a few hours. There are many versions of what actually happened on that night, but Dad was on duty and his story was that the local residents were going down to the platforms where they would spend the night as usual when the sirens sounded. Somebody at the back of the stream of people shone a torch which, along with the noise of the anti-aircraft guns, caused a panic. People at the front were pushed to the ground and were trampled to death by those behind. Of the 2,000 people in the shelter that night, over 170, including forty children, lost their lives. Dad came home the following evening in a state of shock and he never understood why there was almost no mention of this disaster in the newspapers. History tells us that the whole incident was hushed up as it was felt that it would damage morale. By the morning there was no sign that anything had happened the previous night. So far as I recall, Dad never mentioned the incident again but he must have had difficulty coping with the memories of that night. He did mention the funerals, which on some days were as many as fifteen. Sadly, my mother was not a sympathetic person and she would have been no help to him.

There were many incidents that were never reported and looking back on those dark days, it is hard to understand how that generation coped with the horrors that they had to confront on a daily and nightly basis. Wives never knew if they would see their husbands again as they left for work and similarly, husbands never knew if their house would still be standing when they got home. There was no such thing as counselling, no welfare state to fall back on; you either worked or you starved.

10

MUM'S WAR EFFORT

As the war progressed the daylight raids seemed to abate but every night the sirens sounded and we would hear the German bombers overhead on their way to London. Although we had an Anderson shelter, we never used it and we would retreat to our sanctuary under the stairs. However, there was no escaping the noise of the local guns, aided by searchlights, sometimes having success but more often inflicting little damage. Thankfully, we felt we were safe in Lewis Villa.

Sometimes shells fell a little too close to home and one morning we awoke to find a large crater in the middle of Springfield Road, which was only a footpath at the bottom of our garden. Its only real function was access to Clive's bungalow and some fields and bungalows opposite. Along came detachments from the Pioneer Corps and the Ordnance Corps to excavate and defuse what they believed to be an unexploded shell. This involved digging out the existing crater to even larger dimensions until they exposed the shell. They closed off the road, which meant that Clive and his family were isolated, although they persuaded Will Buckley to open a path through his farm to the main road.

My mother came into her own as we were the nearest house and she laid on a constant supply of tea and sandwiches. She loved having strapping young men about the house and I am sure she caused a simple job to take twice as long as a result of her hospitality.

On more than one occasion I would come home from school to find an Army lorry outside the house and a number of soldiers in the house being entertained to tea and homemade cake. It all started when a lorry drew up as Mum was walking home one day and one of the soldiers asked if there was a cafe in the area. This was probably on old trick which she fell for and invited them in. The word must have got around and this hospitality was repeated at least once a week. Mum considered it her contribution to the war effort. I can't imagine what the neighbours thought.

Due to the juxtaposition of the properties owned by JL, our next door but one neighbours in Selena actually had a garden which adjoined ours at the back. They were Mr and Mrs Metcalfe. She originated from Sheffield and he came from North London. In those days there was much formality, particularly amongst the women, and first names were rarely used. Although my mother and Mrs Metcalfe were friends, it was always Mrs Wood and Mrs Metcalfe. I don't think we ever knew her first name. She had an intriguing, rural northern dialect and I learned the meaning of such strange expressions as 'mashing the tea' (brewing tea) and 'mithering' (nagging or scolding someone). The Metcalfes seemed to earn their living from their market garden. They sold vegetables from a shed in their garden and once a week they would deliver orders to their regular customers who patronised the Bull, our local public house. Their method of transporting these orders was unique; an old bicycle had been acquired from which the pedals, chain and chain wheel had been removed. To what was left of the cycle were attached a number of bags and sacks and they would then push the machine the mile to the pub. Mr Metcalfe probably received a pension from the Army as one of his arms was injured. He was a very gentle man and I spent a lot of time helping him in his garden. She was of a different calibre and quite fiery. Inevitably the women fell out but that was some years off. For the present they were our friendly neighbours.

As I think about the toys that we bought for my children and what they buy for their children, it is hard to realise that as a child I had virtually no toys. There were two reasons for this; firstly my mother did not agree with spending money on children's toys. All she was interested in was clothes, which meant that every birthday and at Christmas I received clothes. The second reason, of course, was that toys were not being manufactured. But they were around and every Christmas when Kitty came to stay with the children she had managed to find at least one toy for each of us. Similarly, Auntie Jane never came to stay without a toy or book for me. Sometimes Dad would help out one of his retailers by moving some old furniture and he always searched these pieces. He would often come home with old books or games. On one occasion he brought two huge volumes of lithographs commemorating the reign of Queen Victoria, which I found fascinating. They must have been thrown out during a house move. They would be a rare find today.

11

THE BLACK MARKET

As the war progressed the black market thrived. Shortages and rationing led to illegal activities; either by finding ways around rationing or through straightforward theft, often by looting bombed-out shops. The authorities took these activities very seriously and severe punishments were imposed on those caught profiteering from wartime deprivation. This did not deter the serious offenders and the yard where Dad's workshop was situated had one unit occupied by two partners in crime, who to the outside world were French polishers. However, they were also quite serious villains and they usually had a part in the lorry thefts or burglaries that took place in the East End. Although my father had no direct involvement in these activities, he was obviously well aware of what went on. As a result, certain items came his way, presumably to ensure his silence. One day he came home with a new suit which was part of a consignment coming from Leeds to various Burton shops in London, but failed to reach their destinations. The only problem was that the suit had no buttons, but that was no difficulty for my mother. Dad wore that suit for a long time and passed it onto me when I grew up. On another occasion he came home with some bottles of port and sherry, the proceeds of a smash and grab at an off-licence. Sadly, when they sampled the contents the bottles contained water. Further examination revealed the word 'dummy' at the back of each bottle. But who was the real dummy?

JL always seemed to surround himself with people who could be useful to him. One such person was a detective inspector at Brixton police station. He used to come and visit Joetta for weekends, sometimes with his family and sometimes alone. He always came to us for a meal and shortly before one visit a lorry load of Greys Cigarettes had disappeared on their way to the docks for shipment to the troops in Egypt. Suddenly Dad had promoted himself from Weights to Greys, so no explanation was necessary. By this time the detective had been promoted to Scotland Yard and when he visited Mum always asked him what particular case he was working on. This time it was, of course, the missing cigarettes. There was a hush in the kitchen as I think my parents wondered if I would say anything but I kept very quiet. What the detective didn't realise was that he was actually smoking the proceeds of that robbery.

One day a wooden case of sultanas came into Dad's possession and he had a bit of a problem getting this home. Firstly, the police or even the wardens could stop and search anyone carrying a suspicious looking package, so dad decided he would carry his parcel home on Saturday as the authorities were not so plentiful or vigilant on weekends or during daylight hours. This led to the second problem; he was meeting Grandma and bringing her home to stay with us. Now Grandma had very strict morals and black marketeering was not something she would have tolerated. Dad met her at Aldgate Station and took her into Lyon's for some lunch. As they were going in he spotted a warden at the door and, thinking rather quickly, he made a great show of helping Grandma in with her case and asked the warden if he would kindly keep an eye on Grandma's things, which by now comprised a suitcase and a rather large parcel. The warden never suspected that a sweet old lady could be carrying anything suspicious! My mother did give some sultanas to Grandma when she went home but never said where they came from. I was sworn to secrecy.

On another occasion Dad had acquired some boy's suits and a length of tweed cloth, but as the stop and search policy was being intensified, he decided he would parcel all this up and post it home. The suits fitted me perfectly and Mum decided she would have a costume made from the length of cloth. Now although Auntie Lill was a dressmaker she hated making clothes for the family, so it was decided to get a tailor in the East End to make what she wanted. His name was Phil Solomons and he traded with his brother from a shop not far from Dad's workshop. She had the usual fittings and it must have been school holidays when she went for the final fitting. We were at the shop first thing in the morning and he said it would be ready for lunchtime. Mum wanted to collect it later in the day but he insisted, saying he was going away that afternoon. Mum thought nothing of it, collected the costume and in the train on the way home was surprised to read in the evening paper that Phil Solomons and his brother had been sent to prison that afternoon for clothing coupon offences.

It was never a dull moment for my father and one day whilst the two 'French polishers' were out, the police raided the premises looking for a consignment of stolen butter. Apparently the routine was to get the senior officer away from the others, fix the bribe and send him away, but Dad didn't know this so he tried to call their bluff by telling them to search. They had no choice and found what they were looking for. Dad was promptly arrested and taken to the police station for questioning. They knew he wasn't involved but put him in a cell for a while then released him on bail. Charlie and George worked their magic, money changed hands and nothing further was heard of the matter. They were not always so lucky because they both went to prison, although not at the same time. These absences put a strain on the partnership and they parted company eventually.

There was a lot of corruption in the police force in those days and I don't think JL's detective friend was immune. He would visit Basildon with some rather odd-looking friends and Dad recognised more than one as of questionable reputation.

Outside Lewis Villa, 1943. From left to right: Auntie Bet, Yvonne Steadman, Auntie Lill, Mum and Dad.

Another of JL's contacts was Douglas Steadman, who was manager of the LCC transport depot in Brixton. He had been seconded to the war damage claims office and he met JL whilst assessing some bomb damage at the garage. He and his family soon became regular visitors to Joetta and two totally different personalities forged what could be called a friendship which lasted for some twelve years. Mrs Steadman was a charming lady and they had two daughters and a son. Berkeley was a pilot and we only saw him once before he was posted to India, where he was killed by terrorists when his plane was shot down just after the end of the war. Dorothy was the older daughter who I believe was married and she only visited once or twice. That left the baby of the family, who was called Yvonne. To a seven or eight-year-old, she was a 'goddess'; she was tall, slim with beautiful hair and she loved horse riding. I am not sure how old she was when she first visited, probably sixteen or seventeen, but she was certainly a favourite with me and, in fact, she was liked by all the family. She was a really accomplished horsewoman and was a regular visitor. However, suddenly her visits stopped for no reason and Mrs Steadman also stopped coming. With hindsight, I think that JL started taking too much of an interest in her. However, Mr Steadman continued to visit and as JL's sight deteriorated he drove him every weekend. It was said that he had been promised to be remembered in JL's will. Sadly, he predeceased JL so we never knew. I used to like talking with Mr Steadman, who was a very interesting and highly educated man.

12

THE YANKS ARRIVE

As a child growing up in the forties I had my fair share of illnesses; measles, chicken pox, German measles and, worst of all, impetigo. This was a nasty complaint usually associated with a lack of cleanliness which my mother objected to most strongly. The doctor thought the likely cause was mixing with another child suffering from the same thing. In those days you had to pay to see a doctor and some families simply couldn't afford the charge of 2s 6d plus the cost of any medication, so they just hoped it would go away. The important thing was isolation from other children and bandaging the affected parts, usually arms and legs. Being off school during term time, my mother thought it safe for me to go out. One day I ran into Ken Robbins who was off school with another nasty complaint, ringworm. This affected the scalp and he was out with his head bandaged under his cap. As we were both off school, we decided to go for a walk together. Inevitably we met the dreaded School Board man and his look of disbelief had to be seen to be believed. First Ken took off his cap to reveal a bandaged head and then I showed him my bandaged arms and legs. We must have looked quite a sight. However, he still wasn't satisfied and insisted on seeing our mothers. Ken's house was the nearest so he was taken there whilst I had to

Uncle Harry (second from right) in Egypt. The ammunition dump blew up shortly afterwards, killing some of his colleagues in the photograph.

wait at the gate until it was my turn. Eventually satisfied, he pedalled off looking for real truants.

Getting about in Basildon relied either on public transport or, for us children, the bicycle. I had learnt to ride whilst we were living at Joetta and eventually I had a rather old bicycle which JL acquired from somewhere. Along with my friends, this was our escape and during the long summer holidays we would go off in the morning and stay out all day. There were no worries about paedophiles, although they probably existed, our parents were just happy to see us out of the way for a few hours. If not out cycling we would walk across the fields on summer evenings and when my evening meal was ready, my mother would stand outside the house and shout my name. Her voice would have put many a parade ground sergeant to shame but I managed not to hear her. My friends all heard her shouting but not me. Somehow I used to get away with this deception.

Unlike the youth of today, we did not hang around on street corners intimidating the local population, we kept ourselves occupied. Crime in Basildon was virtually nonexistent, to the extent that almost nobody locked their back door. In fact, all the time we lived at Lewis Villa we did not have a back door key. We would go away for the day and, after the war, on holiday with no security whatsoever. I think the only misdemeanour I can recall is when we went 'scrumping'. That really was ridiculous; with our large orchard the last thing I needed to do was steal fruit, but it was a bit of an adventure.

So, how did we keep out of mischief? We played football, cricket and, to a limited extent, tennis; not an easy task with sports equipment not really available in the shops and no money to buy such things. We scrounged where we could; I persuaded Lew to 'lend' me his cricket bat, and Dave Wenham's father made some stumps so we could play cricket. There was no shortage of land on which to play, although the ground was very rough which made bowling rather erratic.

Uncle Harry sent me a football one Christmas, all the way from Egypt. This arrived around June so we had to wait until the end of the cricket season to enjoy some real football. The problem was that the type of football in use then had a leather case and inside was a bladder which was made of rubber and had to be inflated. This was carried out with a bicycle pump, with the bladder inside the leather ball. Once up to the correct pressure, the whole thing was secured by lacing the aperture. Quite an awkward process. It was not helped by the bladder having suffered the rigours of the Middle East heat and the lengthy transit, which resulted in punctures on a regular basis until we managed to locate a new bladder.

The author on the bike he 'rode' down the stairs in 1942.

Tennis was more complicated. I had acquired two rackets which had belonged to Auntie Bet. They were wooden framed and very warped. One had also lost about half of its strings. Our front lawn was the size of a tennis court but there were two problems. Right in the middle of the lawn was a flower bed and the lawn sloped quite severely. Being resourceful, we were up to the challenge; we played across the lawn. We didn't have a net but I 'liberated' mum's washing line, which had to suffice. She wasn't too pleased when she went to hang some washing out. All this gave me something of an advantage in the gang; upset me and I take my ball or bat home.

For some reason there was a period when I did not use my bicycle; I think it needed a new tyre and it was put upstairs in one of the unused rooms. One day Dad told me to bring it down and he would repair it for me. Auntie Jane was staying with us at the time and she and my mother were talking in the kitchen. I got the bike to the top of the stairs and some crazy idea inspired me into deciding that the easiest way to get it downstairs was to ride it. I have no idea what happened next as all I remember was being at the foot of the stairs with my legs tangled up in the frame. The front door was at the bottom of the stairs and if that had been open, goodness knows where I would have ended up. Hearing my cries, my mother and Auntie Jane came running from the kitchen and just stood looking at my plight and laughing. Whilst I was not in pain, my dignity had been severely hurt and I looked up at Auntie Jane and said, 'Call yourself a nurse, how can you laugh when I am injured?' This just provoked more laughter but eventually they disentangled me from the bike. Of course, the story had to be repeated to Dad when he got home which resulted in more laughter. However, the bike was put right and I was mobile again.

By this stage of the war we had settled into a routine of waiting for the siren, going under the stairs and back to bed when the all-clear sounded. This could happen two or three times a night but the grown-ups just accepted it and got on with their lives.

All through 1940 and 1941 the news in the papers and on the radio had been depressing; the whole of Europe from the Russian front in the east to the Atlantic coast in the west was under German domination, and we had been defeated by the Japanese in most of the Far East. The only high points had been the evacuation from Dunkirk in May 1940 and the Battle of Britain. Although Dunkirk was a defeat, it had somehow been turned into a victory, and the Battle of Britain had thwarted the attempt by the Germans to destroy our air force. Had they succeeded, the invasion of Britain would have followed very quickly. Instead, the Germans turned their attention to the east and in June 1941 launched their offensive against Russia.

By 1942 the news was becoming a little more optimistic. Following the Japanese air attack on Pearl Harbour, the Americans had declared war on Japan and this was closely followed by Germany declaring war on America. Now we really had a world war. The German Navy wasted no time in ordering submarine attacks on United States shipping off the east coast of America.

In the meantime, our run of defeats in North Africa was beginning to be reversed. Rommel had been appointed to command the Afrika Corps and had a few successes, amongst them the recapture of Tobruk. However, in July 1942, General Montgomery was placed in command of our Eighth Army and within three months he had decisively won the Battle of El Alamein, probably a turning point in the North African campaign. These events were reflected not only in the newspapers and on the radio, but also in the cinema newsreels. If a picture of the King, Winston Churchill or General Montgomery was shown on the screen there would be a spontaneous outbreak of applause.

With this degree of optimism, families started to drift back to London and the aunts, possibly motivated by the presence of the American servicemen, were no exception. Through the influence of JL, the aunts had purchased a house in Trent Road in Brixton, just two roads up from Hayter Road. This was a large house divided into two flats, with tenants occupying two rooms on the top floor of the house. The house had basic amenities and I remember the bath was in a cupboard in the kitchen. A new type of shelter was being installed at this time. Called the Morrison shelter, it comprised a large steel table with the underneath fitted with strong steel grille panels which were removable. Its purpose was that mattresses were put under the table where the family would sleep and hopefully be safe from all but a direct hit. Auntie Lill loved the shelter as it provided a huge cutting table for her dressmaking.

Compared to the drab khaki of our soldiers, the smart American gabardine uniforms must have been an irresistible attraction to the ladies, both young and old. The Yanks had money, chewing gum, chocolates, cigarettes and, best of all, nylon stockings. As the war had progressed the availability of silk stockings had almost totally dried up leaving those made of lisle, which most young women would not wear at any price. As an alternative they would paint a dark line up the back of their legs with gravy browning to give the impression that they were wearing stockings. This was fine until their legs got wet and a neat brown line would be transformed into a humiliating and nasty looking brown smudge. Seamless stockings were unknown in those days.

Apparently a pair of nylons could procure just about anything, which probably resulted in a large number of unwanted pregnancies, which was not viewed then as in today's more relaxed climate. Also, most people's perception of the American way of life was gained from the cinema which meant that it was assumed that every one of these young men in their smart uniforms was either a film star or the owner of a huge ranch in Texas. Sadly, the truth was that many of them came from very poor and deprived communities. But the young women of the time were unaware of this, leading to great disappointment after the war when, as GI brides, they went to America and discovered the truth. This sadly resulted in divorces and many an unhappy return to this country.

13

MY FIRST FRENCH LESSONS

I am not sure if the aunts ever slept in the Morrison shelter but their stay in London was short-lived. The house received some bomb damage and it wasn't long before they were back in Basildon. This time they all moved in with us. Grandpa had the spare bedroom downstairs and the rest of us slept in the other room. There was a large divan on which the aunts slept and Mum, Dad and I were in the double bed. It wasn't an ideal situation but this was wartime; modesty gave way to practicality. Auntie Bet commuted to London with Dad every day and Auntie Lill went to London two or three times a week. This created problems in the morning as they all had to be outside the house by 6.30 a.m. to catch the workmen's bus. With only one bathroom and two aunts who took a very long time over their appearance, poor Dad was beside himself every morning and resorted to shaving in the kitchen the night before just to ease the congestion.

During 1942 and 1943 the bombing in London seemed to see-saw and the aunts would be with us for a while and then move back to London for a spell and then back to Basildon. It wasn't ideal for any of us but this was war.

The government was always coming up with new ideas to keep our spirits up and maintain some sort of optimism. In April we would celebrate Empire Day, when all the children who were Scouts or Guides would come to school in their respective uniforms. The Union Jack would flutter from the flagpole in the play ground and we would all sing 'Land of Hope and Glory'. Even I was allowed to sing without censure from Mr Scorer. After the war this was considered politically incorrect and it became Commonwealth Day. How I envied those Boy Scouts in their uniforms and I wished my dad would relent and let me join, but he never did.

We were constantly being urged to put our spare money into National Savings, and it was possible to buy saving stamps which could then be converted into 15s savings certificates. One year, the local schools ran a competition in which the children had to paint a poster; the best three would win saving stamps and their posters would be used in a promotional campaign. My artistic abilities were somewhat below zero, so imagine my surprise when my entry came third. I think I won about 5s worth of savings stamps, but I never remember seeing my poster displayed.

At around this time my mother decided I needed a pet. Although I had never expressed any such interest, I was soon the proud, if somewhat dubious, owner of a puppy which Mum called Paddy. This came via JL, who insisted it had a pedigree 'as long as his arm', although we never actually saw any proof of his breeding. Every so often JL would pat his jacket and assure us that he had the pedigree in his pocket, but somehow we never saw it. He was definitely a mongrel without pedigree and his behaviour was terrible. I knew nothing about training a dog and he lived in a kennel outside our back door. He would bark incessantly, sometimes keeping us awake for hours. I used to take him for walks but he would always run off and come home in his own time. His one endearing feature was that every evening he would lick the glue off the bottom of dad's trousers, presumably because it contained fish extract. In those days, cabinet makers used a fish glue with a distinctive smell, and it quite often got on the clothes of the workers. One Saturday Auntie Bet and I headed into Pitsea and we must have missed the bus because we walked in.

We thought we had left Paddy chained up at home but he must have got free and followed us. We had nothing with us to keep him under control and he was darting from one side of the road to the other with the inevitable result. Along came a bus and Paddy went straight under it. He was killed instantly and the driver just threw his body into a ditch beside the road. We were devastated and went home in tears. My mother was not one to show emotion over such things and she was probably secretly quite relieved. However, we still had to tell Dad. It was agreed that nothing would be said until he had eaten his evening meal. Nobody could pluck up the courage to say anything but suddenly Dad noticed that Paddy wasn't licking his trousers. He asked where Paddy was; Auntie Bet rushed out of the room, I burst into tears and Mum had to tell him the sad news. He was really cut up and wanted to go off to recover his body but by now it was dark and with no street lights it would have been impossible. I must have cared for Paddy more than I realised because I cried myself to sleep for about a week. There was never any mention of pets again.

During the late summer of 1943 we had a particularly bad raid. The aunts and Grandpa were in London, so it was just the three of us. By the early hours of Friday morning we seemed to be under a really heavy attack and suddenly we heard a bomb that Mum and Dad were certain was coming straight for us. For some reason we were not in our usual refuge under the stairs. As they heard the whistle of the falling bomb they both threw themselves on top of me, thinking that at least they would try to ensure my survival. Being half asleep, I fought my way out from under them but by this time the threat had passed; the bomb had missed us and it was not until the morning that we learnt what had happened. All the bungalows in Gordon Road about half a mile from us were constructed of wood and asbestos, which meant that when a single bomb hit one bungalow, about five or six either side just fell down. Only one person was killed, Sylvia, who sat next to me in school. Apparently the family were in the Anderson shelter but the front cover was not in place. Sylvia was looking out at the sky lit up by the searchlights and tracers and she was killed by the blast.

She was a lovely girl and when I started work in London some years later, I used to travel with her older sister who had a wonderful personality and I am sure Sylvia would have grown up to be the same. In school when our teacher asked where Sylvia was, someone said almost casually, 'She was killed last night, Miss'. Then we got on with our lessons. Sadly, death and injury were part of our everyday lives. Again, we couldn't resort to counselling or psychiatric help.

On the following day, which was a Friday, my mother had a visit from the billeting officer whose job was to find accommodation for families who were homeless. There was no option in this; if you had a spare room, it was requisitioned. We had a spare downstairs room that was Grandpa's when he was with us. We were required to put up Mignonne Waters, a single lady who had previously worked for a shipping agent in the City of London. She cared for her father who was billeted next door with the Pulfords at Basildon Stores. They were an interesting pair; Mr Waters was an ex-London policeman whose area was a part of the East End where my mother lived as a child. Prior to that he served in the 9th Lancers in the Boer War and also the First World War. He could certainly tell some interesting stories.

The next day Mr Waters asked my mother if I could go with him to salvage what was left of their possessions. She wasn't too happy but finally agreed. To me it was a great adventure with no thought of the danger of rooting around in what was left of their home. We managed to retrieve quite a lot and it was agreed that we would let them use one of the upstairs bedrooms to store everything.

Mignonne had a dog which my mother swore was a rat but she insisted was a Manchester terrier. Mum wasn't a dog-lover but tolerated this animal. What she was most unhappy about was that Mignonne had the dog in bed with her every night. To my mother, dogs belonged outside in a kennel.

The routine with the Waters was that he slept next door but they both took their meals with us. This was alright for a while but the novelty soon wore off and hostility crept in. Mum felt the Pulfords had got the best of the deal but there was nothing that could be done unless they could find some alternative accommodation, which was clearly not an option. So we were stuck with our uninvited guests, the only consolation being the small amount we were paid by the government and whatever the Waters paid for their food.

In a desperate bid to solve the crisis, my parents offered Mignonne one of the upstairs bedrooms as a bedsit in which she could sleep and cook meals for her father and herself with a small electric stove. She had to collect water from the kitchen and dispose of the waste water but it gave them a degree of independence. We had an unused outdoor toilet and although it had no water, JL installed a toilet pan which was connected to the sewer. Flushing was by taking water from a large, outside rainwater tank and pouring a bucketful into the pan. Not ideal, but again it was independence.

This arrangement was none too soon as the bombing in London suddenly intensified and the aunts and Grandpa returned to Basildon. The aunts had expanded their property portfolio again with the help of JL before the bombing worsened. Auntie Lill bought a house in Horsford Road which ran at the back of Hayter Road. The house was occupied by tenants and was bought as an investment. Meanwhile Auntie Bet had bought a house in Sudbourne Road, on the other side of the school to Hayter Road. By the standards of those days, this was a very modern house with a very up to date bathroom and kitchen. It had three upstairs bedrooms, one for Grandpa, one for the aunts and the third as Auntie Lill's workroom. She worked alone now as her main assistant, Minnie Levy, had joined the ATS.

Grandpa was back in the spare room downstairs and the rest of us were in the other bedroom with Mignonne upstairs. Depending on the severity of the bombing, the aunts would either stay in London during the week or stay with us, with Auntie Bet commuting to London every day with Dad. When they stayed in London during the week there were two bonuses for me. Firstly, on Saturday mornings after Dad had gone to work, Mum would bring us tea in bed and Auntie Lill would recount the film she had seen during the week. She, like all the family, had an almost photographic memory and could recall the whole film in detail. Even to this day if one of these old films is on television, I can remember the story as if I had seen it all those years ago.

The other bonus was that Auntie Lill had enrolled at a local evening class in Brixton to learn French. I think she still yearned for those bronzed young men she had met in the south of France in 1939. On the weekends I would learn the same lesson as she had been taught during the week. Imagine my surprise when I moved on to grammar school in 1945 to find we were working from the same textbook. It gave me a flying start and French was one of the few subjects that I really enjoyed and excelled at.

Looking back, Auntie Lill was very caring towards me. She seemed to have infinite patience from those early days when she helped me to learn to read, she taught me how her sewing machine operated, spent time with me when I was learning to ride a bike and, of course, the French lessons. Even to this day, now she is well into her nineties, she still takes a great interest in me and my family.

During the quieter periods of the war, when the aunts were living in London, one of our Saturday outings was to visit them. It wasn't terribly interesting for me so Dad used to take me with him to work. I really enjoyed those days and they started with a walk down Houndstitch to Liverpool Street, where we stopped for tea and toast. Then on to a No. 8 bus to Shoreditch Church. From there we walked down Valance Road, which comprised a long row of terraced houses, most of which had immaculately whitened doorsteps. On almost every Saturday there was one lady busily working on her step and Dad always raised his hat and said 'Good morning'. When I asked who the lady was, Dad replied that she was Mrs Kray. The name meant nothing to me then but the whole country knew the name many years later.

Dad's workshop was in a yard with various occupants. On the left was a haulage yard and on the right a small house, behind which was a large building housing costermongers barrows. The barrows were the principle means of transporting small loads around the area. Dad used such barrows to take timber to the saw mill or the turner. As we approached the yard, Dad would caution me to be very quiet and we crept past the barrow lady's house. The simple reason for this was that he always owed money for barrow hire and she would chase after him for payment.

Once we had run the gauntlet of the barrow lady, it was upstairs to Dad's workshop, which was like an Aladdin's cave to me. But best of all was the smell, a combination of sawdust and glue. I used to love that smell and if I go into a woodworking premises today I am immediately transported back to Gossett Street.

Saturday for Dad was delivery day and he would hire a Luton van and driver which we would load in reverse order and then we would set off, usually to the area around Kensington. By this time the government had introduced specific designs for 'utility' furniture. The designs were very basic and there were limits on size, number of handles, etc. These restrictions created a challenge to make articles that complied with the rules but looked different. It was a tribute to Dad's artistry that he usually managed to succeed, making his furniture popular with his shop-owning customers. Dad's problem was that he was not a businessman and could not bring himself to charge an adequate price, which was to prove his downfall years later.

Inevitably, one of the retailers would ask us to make a delivery for him and I always enjoyed these because we were delivering in quite an affluent area and there was always a good tip, which Dad gave to me. After the deliveries it was back to Gossett Street by about lunchtime to get cleaned up before making our way over to Brixton. The trouble with that arrangement was that the aunts always had a number of jobs lined up for Dad and he wasn't always too happy about this. As a result he would take me for lunch first and then ask me to choose where I wanted to go. He was happy to take me wherever I wanted to go and we visited the Tower of London, Tower Bridge, St Paul's, as far as the damage allowed, and the only time he refused was when I wanted to climb to the top of the Monument. Sometimes we would just walk round the city, with Dad pointing out well-known landmarks. Eventually we would turn up at Brixton, by which time it was usually too late for any DIY jobs. My mother wasn't too happy about this and for the next few visits we had to go straight to Brixton after lunch.

In the evening we would make our way to Fenchurch Street Station and catch the train home. Travelling by train at night was not without its problems as all the stations were blacked out and it was easy to get off at the wrong place. I am not sure how they got it right, presumably there were landmarks or perhaps they counted the stops. Most commuters during the week would fall asleep on the train and if Alf Buckley, who worked at the Ford factory at Dagenham, happened to get into Dad's compartment, some sort of practical joke was usually planned. Sometimes they would tie Alf's shoelaces together or, worse still, Dad would shake him as the train arrived at Laindon Station, one before Pitsea, and Alf would jump up and be on the platform before he realised he was at the wrong station. Sometimes he managed to get back on the train, sometimes not. Another little ruse was to fool the ticket collector, who was working in the dark, with anything but the return ticket. The usual substitute was a tram ticket, which I suppose in those dark days gave everybody a lift. If there was an air raid during the journey the train would stop and the very dim lights were switched off. I assume the boiler was damped down until the raid was over. I do not remember this happening very often.

Although the news was generally upbeat in the newspapers, the raids were continuing and every day brought more news of devastation in London. Morale was high thanks in part to the King and Queen visiting recently bombed areas, but there were individual and personal tragedies.

One evening Auntie Bet came home in a state of great distress. The garage had been bombed the previous night and staff had been killed. One of the victims was a taxi driver known to all of us; he and his wife had been frequent visitors. It wasn't so much that he had been killed but his head had been severed from his body and it took the staff all day to find it. Poor Auntie Bet just sat and sobbed the whole evening. This was the difference between reading statistics in the newspapers and the reality when tragedy struck close to home.

On another evening Dad told us that one of the drivers from the haulage yard had been close to a bomb explosion, resulting in his windscreen imploding and him swallowing most of the glass. He stayed at work for several weeks after the incident but the end was inevitable and he died about two months later, presumably as a result of internal bleeding.

There was always some excitement to keep us from getting bored and just after harvest time in 1943 we suddenly noticed smoke coming from one of JL's fields. Somebody had set fire to one of the hay stacks. The fire brigade arrived and commenced the task of not only putting the fire out but preventing it spreading to the adjoining hay stacks. The brigade was there all day Saturday and this seemed the time when the requisitioned swimming pool would have a use. Sadly, they discovered it was full of decayed leaves from the overhanging trees which had blocked the filter, making it totally unusable. Fortunately there was a mains supply and eventually the blaze was brought under control. True to form, my mother provided refreshments.

As with every Christmas, in 1943 Kitty came with Doris and Alan and the talk was of the forthcoming 'second front'. Another factor crept into our family celebrations. During the summer we had been successful in getting a telephone and we were now the only house in Basildon with one; even the shop next door was not connected.

Suddenly that Christmas we received calls from a man asking for Kitty. My mother, who considered herself the guardian of the family's morals, said that there was nobody of that name living there. Sadly, as was the case with so many lonely wives, Kitty had taken up with a soldier who was stationed in Melton Mowbray where they were living. She had given him our number for whatever reason. I don't know what happened at that time but my mother's action did not dampen the romance, which eventually led to the break-up of the marriage.

14

I MEET THE ENEMY

As we moved into 1944 the news was coming through that our troops, along with the Americans, were advancing up through Italy and there was speculation about an early invasion of northern France, although that was still some months away.

It was clear to everybody that the invasion was not far off; troops were everywhere and there were massed movements of men and equipment all heading south. Telephone communication was almost impossible and on the south coast all available vacant properties were requisitioned as officer's quarters or offices. The air raids continued to be just as severe, but somehow they didn't seem to matter so much; everybody seemed to sense that victory was coming.

Eventually, on 6 June 1944, came the announcement by American General Eisenhower that we had all been waiting for: Allied troops had landed in Normandy and already towns had been liberated. There was great optimism in the newspapers and on the radio and everybody seemed to think the war would be over by Christmas. Where had we heard that before? It was at about this time that it was felt safe to give up carrying gas masks and that one event seemed to boost morale all round.

But to think that Hitler's Germany was beaten was far too optimistic; he still had a few surprises up his sleeve. The first of these was the V1, or flying bomb. This was a pilotless craft launched from a platform in northern France and carrying sufficient fuel to reach London. Once the fuel ran out the engine cut and the flying bomb fell to the ground with devastating results. These devices were nicknamed 'doodlebugs' because of the awful noise of their engine. They used to fly quite low and slow so they could be seen from the ground and then there was the terrible silence when the engine cut out and people would watch, mesmerised, as it fell out of the sky. These devices were a huge blow to morale just at the time when the news from France was so encouraging. The anti-aircraft guns and fighters had some success but on the whole the majority got through.

The upside, if there was one, was that the blackout was rather superfluous, so it was downgraded to a 'dim out' which meant the total blackout was relaxed and it was permissible to show some light. Strangely enough this did not make much difference because the government had introduced double summer time to help with the harvest during the summer months. This meant that for about eight weeks clocks were put forward two hours, resulting in daylight until around eleven o'clock at night. Of course, it was dark in the morning until around nine o'clock but that was a small price to pay for the long, light evenings. It wasn't easy for parents because children didn't want to go to bed in the daylight.

At about this time we suddenly became aware of German prisoners of war being used to work on the land. Naturally we kids were curious to look at these men who we were assured had square heads and were our sworn enemies. We were soon disillusioned; there were no square heads and they looked just like us. They were also wearing British battle dress and could only be identified by the different coloured patches stitched onto their uniforms. At first we were uncertain how to approach them, but eventually curiosity overcame apprehension and we were quite surprised that some of them spoke English. Because of Grandpa I was quite accustomed to hearing broken English, so I could understand them better than my friends. These were not the wicked enemy we had been brought up to fear and hate. This was very difficult for a nine-year-old to understand. I went home at lunchtime and told my mother about the prisoners, expecting her to forbid me to go near them but, always contrary, she did not object. In fact she taught me a few questions to ask them in what she said was German, but was in fact Yiddish. Unfortunately she did not tell me how to translate the answers but they were impressed with my efforts. One prisoner in particular, Fritz, was very friendly and actually taught me to drive a tractor. This was something that I decided had to be kept to myself. As always, Mum supplied refreshments which were greatly appreciated. I often wondered why the prisoners did not try to escape; they were not guarded and were dropped off and collected by lorry each day. I suppose they were quite happy to stay as prisoners rather than try to return to Germany with a possible posting to the greatly feared Eastern Front.

Bombing raids at this time were sporadic as the Germans were now relying on the V1 bombs. In France, the race was on to find the launch pads which were well defended and not easy to trace from the air.

15

THE HORRORS OF BELSEN

At the same time as our advance into France, the Russians had
turned the tide in the east. Defence suddenly changed to attack
and one of their early successes in July was the recapture of Minsk.
There was some joy in this news but the family were certain that
their relations had perished in what was later to become known as
the Holocaust. What nobody knew until well after the war was that
Stalin's treatment of the Jews in Russia was far more brutal than
that of the Germans. It is possible therefore that the Russian family
had been killed even before the Germans captured Minsk. Sadly we
will never know and because there were discrepancies in spelling
surnames, many of which were Anglicised, it is impossible to establish
the spelling of the names in Russia. Not only were the immigrants
illiterate but the port officials were no better and wrote down what
they thought they heard. This is why so many immigrants ended up
with names such as Sunshine or Sugarman.

This was a busy time in Europe and the news in the papers and on
the radio was of a progressive march across France, with the major
highlight being the Liberation of Paris with General de Gaulle's historic
march down the Champs-Élysées at the head of the French troops.
This was swiftly followed by the Liberation of Brussels and Antwerp.

Whilst all this was going on there was an abortive assassination attempt on Hitler, with terrible repercussions for the perpetrators.

But other more horrific stories were coming out of Europe, the most horrendous being the liberation of the concentration camp at Belsen. The British public were sickened at the photographs being published in the newspapers and seen on the cinema newsreels. Nothing so nauseating and loathsome had ever happened in modern memory and day after day we were shown pictures of piles of skeletons that had once been human beings. The adults found it impossible to comprehend how a supposedly civilised people could commit these unspeakable atrocities against fellow human beings. Also uppermost in the mind of my family, and possibly many Jewish families, was that only a twenty-mile stretch of water had saved us from being part of that pile of skeletons. Sadly, despite the liberation, many inmates were too ill to survive and the death toll continued to rise for some time. Knowing how history could so easily distort historical facts, the American commander who liberated Belsen brought the local German population, led by the mayor, to the camp, not only to witness the horror but to dig graves. In spite of that and all the attendant publicity as further camps were liberated, there are still those today who allege that the Holocaust never happened.

With one last throw of the dice the Germans launched the Battle of the Bulge in mid-December. This took place in the Ardennes on the French–Belgian border and very nearly succeeded in throwing our troops back to the coast. This battle raged for about a month before the Germans were defeated, but it was a hard-fought battle and cost a huge number of lives on both sides. Had the Germans succeeded in this offensive, the whole course of the war in the west would have been drastically altered.

Although the news from the Continent was encouraging, things were not so good in London and the aunts' house had suffered some blast damage, mainly broken windows and damaged roof tiles. It was sad that the beautiful leaded lights were all destroyed and replaced by frosted glass. They carried on in London for a while but eventually they had to succumb and return to Basildon. This made family life in Lewis Villa rather cramped once again. But by now we were becoming used to the difficult domestic arrangements. The difference this time was that we knew it was not going to last much longer. We still had Mignonne living in one room upstairs and her father sleeping at the shop next door. She had utilised many of the possessions recovered from their bombed-out bungalow and the room was quite cosy, with a folding bed for use at night and the small electric cooker for preparing meals. There was a wash stand and Mr Waters used to draw water from the fresh water tank outside the house and carry it up. He disposed of the waste water in the outside toilet. This cosiness did not make my mother too happy, as she felt they were far too comfortable and needed the odd nudge to encourage them to look for alternative accommodation. However, we hardly saw them from one day to the next. Also, we had no choice as the local authority had requisitioned the accommodation.

This left us with the ground floor and we put Grandpa back in the front spare room with the rest of us in the other front room. Fortunately it was a big room but once again privacy was at a premium. Auntie Bet commuted to London daily with Dad and Auntie Lill went back once or twice a week. Poor Dad had the usual problem with Auntie Bet and the bathroom in the morning, but she wouldn't change so he just had to put up with it. What really aggravated him was that on Sundays neither of the aunts bothered to get dressed until after lunch and they would wander about the house in dressing gowns. Sometimes they wouldn't get dressed at all. This was nothing to do with the war and they continued this habit into old age.

We hoped that Christmas 1944 would be the last of the war and there was an air of celebration everywhere. Dad's oldest brother, Fred, had been widowed and he came up from Bournemouth to stay and, of course, Kitty and the children as well. The aunts had returned to London with Grandpa for a while so we had some space. Uncle Fred went in the spare room with the rest of us in the front room. Once again Kitty came up trumps with presents and we had stockings containing such things as sweets, coal wrapped in silver paper and a few little toys. We had made decorations for the house from strips of newspaper held together with glue made from flour and water and everything was as festive as it could be in wartime Britain. Dad wasn't too happy at having a full house but the rest of us had a great time. Uncle Fred was quite a character. He worked in an off-licence in Bournemouth which ensured a reasonable supply of alcohol. Fred liked his drink and, looking back, I don't think he was ever totally sober. Within hours of arriving at Basildon he had visited three of the pubs within walking distance and sampled the beer in each of them. On future visits he would take several hours to travel the three miles from Pitsea Station.

As we progressed into 1945 the end was clearly not far off, another menace invaded our air space. This was the V2 rocket, a deadly weapon which, unlike the V1, gave no warning of its approach and the first indication of its presence was a devastating explosion. In many ways this was the most terrifying of all the aerial weapons and one can only speculate about how the course of the war would have changed if it had been brought into service earlier. To my knowledge, the government had given us no warning of this new weapon. One Saturday morning we were in bed enjoying Auntie Lill recounting the film she had seen during the week when suddenly there was an enormous explosion. This shattered a few windows and one of the chimneys collapsed, dislodging some tiles. We were puzzled as there had been no warning siren and we thought there might have been an explosion at a local ammunition dump. During the day the full story emerged; the rocket had landed in Rectory Road, causing severe damage to the rectory and some of the surrounding houses. Our house was one of many to sustain some damage, but bearing in mind the rectory was almost a mile away, this was frightening news. I think that was the last time Basildon suffered any bomb damage but the raids on London continued relentlessly until our troops located and destroyed the launch sites. This was no easy task as these launch sites were mobile and constantly on the move, unlike those of the V1. After that the skies belonged to us and our allies and everyone wondered how much longer we would have to wait for victory in Europe.

However, before we could get too excited about the end of the war, some of my friends and I had to endure the eleven-plus examination. One Friday morning in late February or early March several of us made our way to Pitsea Primary School to sit a series of papers. My day got off to a bad start as I realised when we were about halfway there that I had forgotten my pen. There were no shops selling them near the school but I need not have worried, the teachers had obviously encountered this problem before and had a supply of spare pens. The upside of sitting the exam was that we finished the exams by lunchtime and had the rest of the day off.

As March gave way to April the news got better and better; the net was closing in on Berlin with the Russians coming from the east and the Allies from the west. Also, our troops had travelled up through Italy and there had been a further approach from the south of France. One by one the news of countries achieving freedom emerged. Sadly things could never go back to the pre-war status quo and there was also news of kings being deposed and so called 'democracies' being established. Old scores were being settled with a terrible degree of violence. In France, Belgium and Holland those known or suspected to have been German collaborators were paraded in the town squares and publicly humiliated, many being stripped naked and having their heads shaved. There were also quite a few summary executions. Even today, over sixty years after the cessation of hostilities, feelings run high in the French villages.

16

VICTORY IN EUROPE

The news of the suicides of Adolf Hitler and Eva Braun on 30 April was greeted with great celebration The war was nearly over. The Allies were insisting on an unconditional surrender, which was finally achieved on 8 May 1945. Flags appeared everywhere and there were street parties in London and the large towns. In our part of Basildon it was rather lower key, with Mr Bland organising a large bonfire with an effigy of Hitler on the top. Sadly, even at this time of great celebration, anti-Semitism reared its ugly head. I cannot remember how it started but it seemed that the whole war had been fought for my personal benefit. I went home in tears and although we had two days off school, for me the edge had been taken off the whole event

As children we all expected things to revert to normal overnight. This was far from the case and, in fact, things were going to get a whole lot worse. Food and fuel shortages became even more severe, worse than during the war. Sweets were still rationed and in short supply, and newsprint was still very scarce so any thoughts of comics being freely available were short-lived.

However, it was not all bad news and one day in late May the postman delivered that much awaited letter from the Education Office telling us that I had passed the eleven-plus. In the hope that I would secure a place at Palmer's School in Grays, I spent hours with my next door neighbour Doug Riley, who had been to Palmers a few years earlier. Doug was Mrs Pullford's grandson and ran the grocery shop. He had been forced to leave school early because her eyesight was failing. It all seemed very exciting and totally different from the type of school I had been used to.

But Palmers was some time away; in the meantime it was easy to forget that it was only in Europe that victory had been achieved. The conflict was being fought ferociously in the Far East on land, sea and in the air. Sadly, wives and parents were still receiving the dreaded telegrams from the War Office and this situation was to continue for another three months.

In theory we had finished our education at Vange School and both Miss Webb and Mr Scorer had to find ways to keep us occupied. Those of us who were going on to grammar schools were separated and taught the basics of algebra and French. Thanks to what I had learned from Auntie Lill the French was easy for me but I never really understood algebra and it was only many, many years later whilst helping my sons with their homework that I finally understood the subject.

Fortunately, we had a good summer and we played a lot of cricket and had the first sports day at the school since before the war. Mr Scorer was very adept at getting the boys to do odd jobs about the school and he soon had us painting the portable blackboards or doing odd gardening jobs. In today's climate he would never had got away with this but we enjoyed being able to ingratiate ourselves with the headmaster.

In June there was great excitement as Winston Churchill had called a general election, the first since before the war and everybody expected an easy Conservative victory. Polling day was set for 8 July and due to the forces' postal votes, it was going to be almost three weeks before the result was known.

17

A Family Crisis
and Churchill Rejected

For us a crisis was looming. My mother had been unwell for some time but, typical of her generation, she was reluctant to see the doctor. We had election day off school as it was being used as a polling station. Early in the morning my mother came into my bedroom and it was clear that she was very ill. I got up and she fell into my bed. At ten years old I didn't really know what to do but I did call the doctor. Before he arrived my mother started to vomit and she was bringing up green fluid, which I knew was bad. Whilst waiting for the doctor I called Mrs Metcalfe, who took one look at her and in her broad Sheffield accent said, 'Eh you do look bad luv, Mrs ... looked just like you just before she died'. Clearly calling her had not been a good idea.

The doctor arrived, examined Mum and left, saying he would return after lunch. By now I was at my wit's end and wanted Dad to come home. There was no way of contacting him by phone so I sent a telegram telling him to come home at once. In the meantime the doctor returned after lunch and decided Mum had to go to hospital. He wanted to go back to his surgery to make the arrangements but I persuaded him to use our phone. Hospital beds were at a premium as most were occupied by wounded servicemen and I remember him shouting down the phone, 'Do you expect me to operate on the patient's dining room table?' Eventually he found a bed and alerted the operating theatre but he never said to which hospital she was going. In no time an ambulance arrived and I did remember to ask the driver where they were headed. Chelmsford, he said, not mentioning that there were two hospitals in Chelmsford. Just as the ambulance set off Dad arrived, but too late to go with Mum. His first task was to phone Auntie Lill and ask if I could go and stay with her and Auntie Bet. Naturally she said yes and a case was packed. Very soon we were off to the station and I was put on the train to be met at Fenchurch Street Station by Auntie Bet. Meanwhile Dad had to make his way to Chelmsford, which was not easy as there was no direct rail or bus link. I think he had to go to Southend and change stations to catch a train to Chelmsford. Having arrived he made for the main hospital only to find that Mum was in a smaller, mainly military, hospital. He arrived after a five or six hour journey and Mum was just being brought back from theatre. He was told that they had removed an ovarian cyst weighing about seven pounds and it was this cyst that had been found by the doctors in Dingley five years before and left untreated.

Having seen my mother carried off in the ambulance so obviously ill I was convinced she would not survive. It was such a joy the following morning when Dad phoned to say that she had come through the operation successfully. At that time with few antibiotics, major operations carried enormous risk of infection and patients were required to stay in hospital for many weeks to recuperate. This meant Dad had to make a difficult journey to Chelmsford every evening after work. Matters were not helped by his tendency to fall asleep on the train, which quite often resulted in him waking up at the end of the line in Colchester and having to catch another train back to Chelmsford, often arriving just as visiting time was over. My mother was not well pleased. One piece of good fortune was that the lady in the next bed, Mrs Bates, was from Pitsea and her husband came to visit by car every evening which meant that Dad was always able to get a lift home.

The aunts were actually booked to go on holiday to Bournemouth on the Saturday after my mother was rushed to hospital and Auntie Jane was on her way to look after Grandpa. She was probably quite pleased to have me in the house for company. Sadly, her culinary skills had not improved over the intervening years but I cannot remember what sort of meals she prepared.

On the Friday morning a phone call to JL got his agreement that I could go to the garage and he arranged to collect me on his way. I suppose it was a good idea to give me a different interest after my ordeal the previous day. JL collected me and his garage was so much larger than I had imagined, with huge workshops plus parking space for up to around 100 cabs. The war damage following the previous bombing had not been repaired and part of the first floor was a vast open expanse. I found a positive side to this in subsequent visits because this area actually overlooked the Oval Cricket Ground and was adjacent to the famous 'gas works end' which meant that I could watch the matches, although from a distance.

On this first visit I met JL's son-in-law, Eddie, who was in charge of the office and also renewed my acquaintance with several of the drivers who had been visitors at Joetta. Amongst them one stands out. He was Archie Whiting, a frequent visitor. His pastime was shooting and he was always dressed in Prince of Wales check plus fours and would prowl along the edges of the fields looking for rabbits or anything that he saw in his sights. Naturally, I was there with him every evening after school and like so many adults that I came into contact with, he taught me a lot about the countryside. I always found it difficult to understand how he could be a London cabbie; to my mind he belonged on a country estate.

Of course Lew was also there and gave me a tour of the premises and introduced me to the mechanics and some of the drivers. I also learned the after-lunch routine of JL, Lew and Eddie. At about 1 p.m. all three were nowhere to be seen. JL would shut himself in his office with the door locked, Lew and Eddie would find a cab at the back of the garage and they would sleep for about an hour. I had never come across anything like this before; in our family you slept at night and worked during the day.

In the mid-1940s hospitals had strict visiting rules and one that was rigorously imposed was that children were not allowed in the wards. After about three weeks Auntie Bet and Jane took me back to Basildon for the weekend so that we could visit my mother on the Sunday. Dad's new friend, Mr Bates, picked us up in his little car; I think there were six of us crammed in, and we set off for Chelmsford Hospital. Most of the wards were single-storey wooden huts, rather like Army barracks, and Dad opened the window behind Mum's bed so that I could climb up outside and speak to her. Surprisingly, we had little to say to each other but she was pleased to see me. Just before visiting was over I slipped into the ward and crept under the beds so that I could kiss Mum goodbye. The other ladies thought this was highly amusing and I managed to get in and out without being caught by the dreaded ward sister.

About two weeks later Mum was ready to be discharged and it was agreed that she would spend two weeks with the aunts in Brixton by way of convalescence. Dad would continue to commute to Basildon and spend some evenings with us.

One surprise was in store for my parents; the bill that was presented to them when Mum was discharged. In those days there was no National Health Service – that was some three years away – and all medical treatment had to be paid for. Also, there would be another bill at home from our GP for the two visits he made on the day Mum was sent to hospital. The hospital authorities were quite understanding and did not insist on payment on discharge, but the bill did have to be paid. I think the total cost including the ambulance, operation and hospital stay was about £30; rather less than private medical treatment today. Our GP charged about 7s 6d for a home visit plus medicine and slightly less if you visited the surgery.

During the aunts' holiday in Bournemouth, Auntie Lill met a very nice American soldier called Charles Gunter – Chuck to everyone – and he was a regular weekend visitor. He never talked about his wartime experiences or indeed his life in America. From the way he enthused over how we lived and JL's car, my mother concluded he was from quite a poor background; she even thought he might have a wife in America. None of this interested me; I was well supplied with candy bars, chewing gum and American magazines. Chuck wasn't around long and was either posted home or to Europe. The promised correspondence between Chuck and Aunt Lill never happened.

The aunts never did housework and at that time they had a lady who 'did' for them, Mrs Gee. When Mum described her operation, her first words were that these growths came back in a short time which was what had happened to one of her friends who had recently died from a similar complaint. My mother certainly proved her wrong by living a further fifty-six years, dying at the great age of ninety-four.

I had noticed over the years that words relating to illness were never spoken out loud. The words such as 'she's got a growth down below' were mouthed and you had to lip-read to understand what was being said. It was almost as if speaking the words out loud would attract the illness to the speaker. I believe such superstitions continue to this day in parts of the north of England.

Facing another two weeks of inactivity in Brixton, I was becoming a bit of a nuisance. I had no friends, no bike, no fields to tramp and not even any of my books to read. Somehow the aunts came up with a solution; I would go to JL's garage with Auntie Bet every day. This was fine by me and I was put in the office with jobs to do rather than just wandering around behind JL. I worked a nine to six day and the part I enjoyed the most was at the end of the day when the drivers brought their takings in to be checked. Each taxi had a meter which was calibrated in pennies and this was checked by the workshop foreman, who would give the driver a form with the reading. I then had to deduct the previous reading which gave me the takings for the day in pennies and which then had to be converted to pounds, shillings and pence. There were no calculators in those days, it was all done by simple arithmetic and having worked out the takings I then had to add up the cash on the counter and hope that the two amounts tallied.

Of course I wasn't allowed to do all this unsupervised; Auntie Bet or Eddie were watching my every move. Looking back, they could probably have done the job much quicker themselves but they were just being kind.

At around this time major events were taking place at home and abroad which would shape history for many generations to come. The first shock to the British people was the defeat of Winston Churchill and the Conservative party at the general election. Thanks mainly to the service vote and the promise that all the troops would be home by Christmas, the Labour Party, led by an almost unknown, Clement Atlee, were swept into power. To me at ten years old, this seemed devastating. Churchill was our hero, the man who had single-handedly saved our country from annihilation by the Germans. How could the British people be so disloyal and stupid? Dad told me not to worry, as the Labour Party had been elected in the mid-1930s and made such a mess of things that they were soon out of office. He predicted the same fate befalling them again. Sadly, he was wrong and they stayed in office for six years.

18

WHERE IS THE 'BRAVE NEW WORLD'?

Although we had peace in Europe, the conflict continued in the Far East. Our troops in the Far East had not received the same coverage in the newspapers as their counterparts in Europe and at one time they were dubbed 'the forgotten army'. The soldiers were subjected to terrible conditions, and in reality they were fighting two enemies; the Japanese soldiers and the hostile jungle in countries such as Burma. Most of the time our soldiers were up to their necks in swamps; conditions that they had never experienced at home and for which they were totally unprepared and untrained. They were struck down by malaria, dysentery and beriberi, for which the medicines available at the time offered very little relief. Added to the horrific conditions was the much-feared Japanese Army. These soldiers came from an alien culture and fought by a totally different set of rules. They were at home in the jungle and would travel round by bicycle, appearing suddenly, inflicting heavy casualties and disappearing back into the jungle. American, British and Commonwealth troops were making progress but it was painfully slow and victory was not just around the corner.

For many years scientists on all sides had been working on a 'super' weapon, something the world had never seen before. This was the atomic bomb and we learned later that the Germans had been very close to manufacturing this bomb towards the end of the war. In the event it was the Americans who won the race and we awoke on 6 August 1945 to the news that the first atomic bomb had been dropped by the Americans on Hiroshima with devastation on a scale never witnessed before. A whole city just disappeared as a result of this one bomb, but still the Japanese would not surrender. Three days later a second atomic bomb was dropped on Nagasaki, with similar results. Surely the Japanese would surrender now. It took another five days but at last, on 14 August 1945, the Japanese surrendered and the Second World War was finally over – five years and eleven months since I had boarded that bus in Catherine Street School playground. On 15 August we celebrated VJ Day and the celebrations really began. All that was missing was our troops, who had been promised a homecoming by Christmas. For many this happened, but not for everyone. The conquered territories had to be administered until a time when it would be possible to hand control back to the local population. And, of course, we still had conscription until the late 1950s.

Just as with Germany, horrific pictures and stories were coming out of Japan. To the Japanese soldiers, surrender was an act of cowardice and Allied prisoners were treated with extreme cruelty by their guards with harsh, sometimes fatal, punishment imposed on miscreants. We also heard a new expression, 'hari-kari', which was a form of suicide. In some instances a group of officers would appoint one of their number to behead his colleagues and then fall on his own sword. Another phenomena unknown in the west were the suicide bombers. Unlike the V1s that were sent over London, these flying bombs, filled with high explosive, were piloted. The pilot was locked in his cockpit with no way to escape. He would then select his target and fly his plane straight at it, exploding on impact. Ships were the main target for these planes. To our European culture these actions were very strange to us and at the time we were filled with a loathing for the Japanese.

But what of Poland, the country we had gone to war to defend? Sadly there was no liberation for the Polish people or indeed most of the Eastern European countries dubbed 'sub-human' by Hitler and his evil henchmen. Instead they became satellites of Stalin's Soviet Union and it would be over fifty years before they would achieve independence. How did this happen? How had cuddly 'Uncle Joe' Stalin suddenly been unmasked as the wicked, sadistic dictator hated by the Western powers?

Several events conspired in Stalin's favour. Firstly, in February 1945, a conference had taken place at Yalta comprising Roosevelt, Churchill and Stalin. Both Roosevelt and Churchill were sick men; the American President had only a few months to live and Churchill had recently suffered a stroke. This gave Stalin the upper hand, resulting in too many concessions being granted to the Soviet Union. It got worse; Roosevelt died in April 1945 and was replaced by an almost unknown, Harry S. Truman. This was followed by Clement Atlee becoming Britain's Prime Minister in July. This left the tough and uncompromising Stalin dealing with two 'lightweight' Western leaders and he exploited their inexperience to his complete advantage.

Of course I understood none of this at the time but, as always, I listened to the grown-ups and, in many ways, the talk around the table was much more interesting after the war, probably because I was older and could understand a lot more of the conversation.

My war ended in Basildon and I was too young then to reflect on how the last five years had affected my life. But, with the benefit of hindsight, I suppose the one unarguable fact was that I grew up at a much faster rate than would have happened if the war had not occurred.

The promised 'Brave New World' did not happen. Food was in even shorter supply than during the war. Even bread and potatoes were rationed and coal supplies were virtually non-existent. We were confronted by strikes and in one of the worst winters of recent times, we were so cold that we had to go to bed in the early evening and electricity was quite often cut off on a rota basis. Hardly the land fit for heroes that our troops had been promised!

As I said earlier, Basildon was not a designated evacuation area which meant that the end of the war did not result in a wholesale exodus back to London. In fact, I cannot remember anyone leaving and we might possibly have been the first family to return to London, but that was not until five years after the war.

I do not think my war was particularly special; we endured our share of the London bombing, lost our house, our home and quite a few friends. Generally we suffered the deprivations that war brings about. Thousands of other children must have had similar experiences. From stories I have read and in conversations, many evacuees had very unpleasant times. I was fortunate that my mother chose to keep me with her; otherwise my war might not have been how it was.

I was also fortunate not only to have the love of my parents but also my aunts around me. It was in this loving environment that I grew from almost a toddler to a well-adjusted ten-year-old. Yes, I may have grown up a little too quickly but nobody escapes the consequences of war. I was one of the lucky ones.

By the end of 1945 both Uncle Harry and Uncle Jack were reunited with their families. We had been fortunate in not losing any family members, but we had lost many friends. In addition we had lost contact with quite a number of pre-war friends. There were many reasons for this; some had left London and stayed away, others had, like us, been bombed out and presumably lost contact addresses. Surprisingly, when we put Grandpa's bereavement announcement in the *Jewish Chronicle* some fourteen years after the end of the war, the family was reunited with some long lost friends.

I think two major factors carried the population through those dark days. Firstly, it was our great British sense of humour. Somehow it rose to the occasion and even during times of great tragedy there was always a humorous element. Secondly, it was the sheer grit and willpower of the civilian population. It would have taken a lot

Lewis Villa after the war, with the shiplap pebble-dashed and the veranda demolished due to bomb blast damage.

to defeat that iron resolve which was determined not to be beaten. Fortunately, it was never put to the test.

What is generally overlooked when recounting the history of the Second World War is that Adolph Hitler did not seize power in Germany; he was appointed Chancellor in January 1933 by the then President, Paul von Hindenburg. Germany was impoverished by the punitive and vindictive terms of the 1919 Treaty of Versailles and the rise of an extreme political faction was inevitable. Whether the politicians learned any lessons, only time would tell. Sadly, it is the general public in each country that ends up paying the ultimate price of these political decisions. It is left to the survivors to rebuild the countries in future years in the wake of such destruction. This is not just rebuilding our beloved countries, but the ultimate goal must be to seek peace. Human nature being what it is, can it ever wholly be achieved?

Other titles published by The History Press

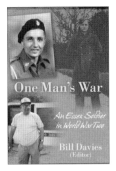

One Man's War: An Essex Soldier in World War Two
BILL DAVIES

A veteran of D-Day, Ron Davies joined the TA before war began and was called up as a tank gunner or 'Bombardier' with the Essex Yeomanry, but D-Day was his first experience of action. This book follows the training and build-up to D-Day, covers the invasion minute-by-minute, and carries on through the Allied push through France, Belgium and Holland. Ron's story continues with the regiment's heartbreaking round of duty at Belsen and following that their continuation to the Baltic Coast.

978 0 7524 4517 5

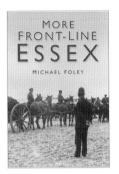

More Front-line Essex
MICHAEL FOLEY

More Front-line Essex provides more evidence that Essex has always been one of the most heavily defended counties in Britain. In order to stop the invasions of the Spanish, the Dutch, the French under Napoleon and the Germans in two world wars, the county became what was essentially an armed camp. This led to the building of defensive positions that have in some cases evolved over a period of 500 years or more to meet the changes in weaponry that have taken place.

978 0 7509 4951 4

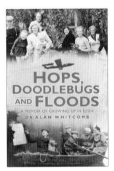

Hops, Doodlebugs and Floods: A Memoir of Growing up in Esssex
DR ALAN WHITCOMB

This is the true tale of a boy born into a typical East End family in the Second World War, beginning with his early memories of hop picking and having little money, and moving on to his life in the 1950s and his experience of the devastating east coast floods of 1953. This is an entertaining, humorous and nostalgic read for anyone who remembers Essex in the Second World War and beyond.

978 0 7524 5181 7

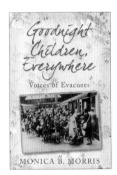

Goodnight Children, Everywhere: Voices of Evacuees
MONICA B. MORRIS

For the many children torn from their families the evacuation at the outbreak of the Second World War was a life-changing experience. In *Goodnight Children, Everywhere*, men and women who were children at the time recall their poignant memories of being labelled, lined up and taken away. Some children were advantaged by the dramatic change in their lives; others, separated from all they knew and loved, suffered unendurable heartbreak. This is their story.

978 0 7524 5282 1

Visit our website and discover thousands of other History Press books.

www.thehistorypress.co.uk